b:report2.fil



# THE COST OF LEARNING WITH COMPUTERS

# The Cost of Learning with Computers

## The Report of the Financial Evaluation of the National Development Programme in Computer Assisted Learning

**J Fielden and P K Pearson**

Peat, Marwick, Mitchell & Co
Management Consultants

CET Council for Educational Technology

Published and distributed by the
Council for Educational Technology
3 Devonshire Street, London W1N 2BA



First published 1978
ISBN 0 902204-77-7

---

BL British Library Cataloguing in Publication Data

---

Fielden, John
The cost of learning with computers.
1. National Development Programme in Computer Assisted Learning
2. Computer-assisted instruction — Great Britain 3. Cost effectiveness
I. Title II. Pearson, PK III. Council for Educational Technology for the United Kingdom
338.4'3 LB1028.5

ISBN 0-902204-77-7

---

Printed in Great Britain by
Thomas Jenkins (Printers) Limited
108 Weston Street, London SE1

# Contents

# Introduction and background

This is the final report from a four-and-a-half-year project concerned with studying the financial and resource implications of more than 30 development projects in a range of education and training establishments. The subject matter of the report covers several innovations, since not only were the educational changes advanced, but also the organizational framework of the funding agency and the very existence of an external financial evaluation function were themselves significant novelties. Thus, we hope that this report will have a wider relevance than simply to the project staff. The problems of measuring the costs and resource implications of educational change are slowly attracting serious study. We believe this report will help to explain one attempt to isolate and measure the impact of such changes. It is not an easy task and there are, we concede, many areas where no precise answer is ever likely to be obtained. We hope however that we have laid the groundwork for other studies in the same genre.

The National Development Programme in Computer Assisted Learning (NDPCAL) was a remarkable innovation in the area of financing educational change. The Department of Education and Science decided to earmark £2 million for testing and developing the use of the computer as an aid to teaching, to be distributed through an independent agency. A small central Directorate was established by Richard Hooper in 1973; its numbers fluctuated, but never exceeded seven people including secretarial support. The overall direction and control of policy remained with a 22-strong Programme Committee which contained representatives of seven government departments and of bodies such as the Council for Educational Technology, Schools Council, University Grants Committee and Social Science Research Council and an important group of coopted advisers from academic, technical and industrial organizations. The Programme Committee received proposals for projects after they had been developed jointly by the Directorate and the project staff; in a few cases submissions put forward were not approved. In the later stages of its life the Committee began to receive evaluation reports on projects and concerned itself with generalizations and conclusions that could be made about computer assisted learning (CAL) and computer managed learning (CML) in the future.

Computer assisted learning is not like programmed learning and computer assisted instruction as practised in the USA. It involves the use of the computer in teaching in a variety of ways: simulation of processes or experiments to increase understanding, 'drill and practice' to help the mastery of technical knowledge, and calculation and analysis facilities. In many instances the computer will be teaching something that cannot be taught in any other way. Computer managed learning involves the use of the computer to help the teacher by undertaking managerial tasks for him such as marking, routing pupils through courses, assessing their progress, recording scores and producing analytical reports on their performance.

At the outset Hooper was concerned about the credibility of the judgements which might be made on the Programme and its success or failure. As he admitted so frankly in *Two Years On,* 'both the staff of the Directorate and even more the project staff have in some senses a career stake in CAL's success' (Hooper, 1975); from these convictions sprang the need for the two independent evaluations of NDPCAL. The major evaluation effort was clearly to be an assessment of the educational impact of NDPCAL. This was carried out by a team led by Barry MacDonald of the Centre for Applied Research in Education at the University of East Anglia, which quickly gave itself the acronym UNCAL (Understanding Computer Assisted Learning). UNCAL's work, which lasted from January 1974 to December 1977 at a total cost of £134,200, has been described by MacDonald in his mid-term and final reports (UNCAL, 1975) (MacDonald *et al,* 1978). During its four-year life the educational evaluation found itself in the centre of several vigorous debates about its rationale and method, but by 1977 it had achieved an understanding with its critics. The UNCAL philosophies of opening up sensitive issues and of trying to meet the information demands of many different levels of audience created conceptual and operational problems for the team, of a kind which we never had to face.

In May 1973 the Programme Committee approved a contract for an independent financial evaluation of all NDPCAL's projects. The rationale was clearly linked to the final words of the Programme's first objective: 'to develop and secure the assimilation of computer assisted and computer managed learning on a regular institutional basis *at reasonable cost'*.

Hooper's personal career experience in educational television had led him to be sceptical about claims for savings arising from the introduction of advanced educational technology. He feared that CAL and CML projects could also mask their resource implications in the same way, unless an authoritative independent evaluation watched them closely. While the idea of such an evaluation contract being granted to run concurrently with the projects was a novelty in the United Kingdom (where financial studies were carried out retrospectively, if at all), there was a recent precedent in the United States of America. In 1973 the National Science Foundation (NSF) contracted with the Educational Testing Service of Princeton to undertake educational, cost and technology evaluations of the PLATO and TICCIT projects. These were the two largest computer-based instructional systems in the USA and their development was largely funded by the NSF. The PLATO IV (Programmed Logic for Automatic Teaching Operations) system involved, in its largest application, 950 terminals controlled by one large computer. The system has been marketed commercially by the Control Data Corporation since 1976 and as a result the cost and technology evaluations were dropped, since their aims had been largely superseded by the commercial takeover. In the case of the TICCIT project, Hazeltine Corporation have taken over the commercial distribution of the materials, so that for the same reason the NSF's cost and technology evaluations were terminated.

Our financial evaluation contract for NDPCAL covered the four-and-a-half-year period from May 1973 to September 1977 and cost a total of £62,545. Until May 1975, John Fielden carried out the work alone; he was then joined by Philip Pearson, since the number of projects commissioned and the resulting workload had considerably exceeded original expectations.

This report presents problems of presentation and structure. The combination of costing and CAL is an unusual one which would hardly appeal to the general reader even in education. However, there are some parts of the story which we believe deserve a wider audience. These are the chapters relating to the work of the evaluation and the problems of undertaking financial analyses of changes in education. In the specialist chapters concerning CAL and CML there is also a conflict between potential readers. Some will want generalizations on broad issues such as costs, computer or development times, while others will be interested in a specific area of application in training or education. Thus, although we have tried in our layout to satisfy most audiences by a combination of approaches, we will inevitably have failed to please some.

Part A of this report contains chapters on general issues related to the Programme; we believe they have a broader relevance and value than the remainder of the report. Chapter 1 describes some of the conceptual and practical problems facing the financial evaluation; many of these will be common to all attempts to cost or measure educational change. Chapter 2 describes in some detail the work of the evaluation and explains what solutions we adopted to the problems we met. The final chapter of this part of the report discusses the claims for managerial innovation that have been made about the Programme and explores the transferability of some of its innovations.

Part B contains our conclusions on NDPCAL. Chapter 4 concerns CAL, firstly in higher education where 62% of NDPCAL's project funds were spent and then in other sectors such as secondary education and training. Chapter 5 covers the CML projects commissioned by the Programme. To a large extent our comments have to be project-specific because the small number of projects (compared with CAL in higher education) in each sector does not allow confident generalizations. This is even more true when we come to Chapter 6 which covers military projects. In the USA there have been several examples of military use of computers which make claims for cost-effectiveness. There are thus particular grounds for our interest in this area. Unfortunately the British military projects were all commissioned at too late a stage in the Programme's life for any conclusions to be drawn as to their long-term financial effect. Chapter 7 examines one of the Programme's principal slogans, its emphasis on transferability of materials and ideas between institutions. We look at the effectiveness of some of the mechanisms which were set up to facilitate this. The final chapter of the report studies some crucial questions. How do CAL and CML compare in cost terms with 'conventional' methods? Is such a comparison relevant? What techniques, if any, can help us to contrast the costs and the outcomes of NDPCAL? Has the nation got value for money?

The appendices attempt partly to remedy one failing of the report, its tendency to generalize and concentrate on broad themes without explaining a real project. Appendix A therefore describes a CAL project, the Computational Physics Teaching Laboratory at the University of Surrey. Appendix B is devoted to the largest operational CML project in the NDPCAL, the Hertfordshire Computer Managed Mathematics project. In Appendix C we describe all the 29 projects which we evaluated and give a small amount of quantitative information about each. Appendix D reverts to the specific theme of our methodology in carrying out the evaluation; it provides a detailed look at some of the working papers and pro-forma we adopted in our work. Appendix E is a brief note on the cost and content of our evaluation, while Appendix F provides references and a bibliography for the whole of our Report.

**Acknowledgements**

Our major thanks must go to the project staff who have, almost without exception, been so conscientious and dedicated in collecting the data which was necessary for our work. In some cases their enthusiasm led them to undertake detailed cost calculations beyond the scale we required. Even though some academic staff were initially suspicious and doubtful about our functions and our procedures, they all cooperated fully with our requests for information at a considerable cost to themselves in time. We are extremely grateful to them.

The staff of the Department of Education and Science and the Council for Educational Technology have been very helpful and cooperative; in particular we thank John Hudson who, as chairman of Programme Committee, allowed us to sit in on all its sessions.

Finally, our thanks to all the staff of NDPCAL itself. They have exhibited unfailing friendliness and assistance and have readily allowed us access to all their files, papers and references. The personal friendships we have built up with NDPCAL's Directorate over the last four years have made our work immensely enjoyable and memorable.

John Fielden
Philip Pearson
Peat, Marwick, Mitchell & Co

# PART A

# 1. Problems of educational cost analysis

## 1. Introduction

The aim of an overall evaluation of the activities of the National Development Programme in Computer Assisted Learning is to answer the questions: when are the long-term cost and resource implications of the various innovations, and, is the expenditure justified by the resulting outcomes or benefits? The main steps in an analytical approach to answering these questions are (i) identifying the changes in input which are necessary (ie, the resources needed) and the resulting changes in outcome (which may have measurable resource effects or may be unquantifiable) (ii) measuring the input and outcomes wherever possible (iii) deciding on the audience for the study; this will normally mean identifying the level at which decisions will be taken on further investment (iv) analysing the data on resources and outcomes; this may involve combining the effects on very different resources measured in a variety of units (v) presenting the results in the best form to aid policy-makers in arriving at a decision on future investment.

This is the approach we have suggested elsewhere (Fielden and Pearson, 1978) for a cost analysis of innovation in education and training; it can often result in a fairly clear-cut decision. This can happen, for example, where the change is introduced to solve a particular organizational problem; here the educational outcome can be assumed to be at least as 'good' as previously and the analysis can concentrate on showing whether the long-term resource implications warrant the initial investment of funds. Alternatively, the aim of the innovation might be to provide educational benefits with no increase in cost — in this case the analysis can identify the changes and verify the long-term effects on resources and the final decision can then be made on purely educational grounds.

In this chapter we discuss the problems in applying this analytical approach to NDPCAL's projects. There are some difficulties in identifying and measuring the costs involved, but the main problem is that neither of the situations outlined above, which allow a fairly definite conclusion to be reached, applies in the educational use of computers. Computer assisted or managed learning almost always results in an extra cost which is not matched by measurable benefits. The main claimed outcomes are normally an improvement in the quality of learning and the methods are often attempting to do things that cannot be achieved by conventional means. The overall assessment therefore becomes one of value judgement, where measured extra resources are set against qualitative claims or predicted benefits and our analysis can only provide part of the answer.

We have attempted to rationalize and quantify wherever possible, but it must be accepted that a large degree of subjective judgement remains and there is no complete answer to the question of 'how much does computer assisted learning cost?' and still less to that of 'is it worth it?' In the long run, the eventual scale of acceptance of any innovation depends on the strength and consistency of the demands made on its behalf for a share of the limited resources available. The strength and success, or otherwise, of these competing claims on national resources are probably themselves the best indicators of the value of any new venture, representing as they do the final *quod erat demonstrandum* in the arithmetic of the unquantifiable.

## 1.2 Identification of change in costs and outputs

The costs of an innovation consist of the extra resources required and the reallocation of existing resources; not all of the costs result in financial outlay. The main components of cost are:

— the capital and recurrent cost of hardware
— the use of computer time on existing installations
— equipment maintenance
— the time of specially recruited or funded staff
— the time of existing staff
— accommodation
— share of overheads and services
— travel, promotion and subsistence expenses

Straightforward as this looks, there are problems of identification. Staff time in total might be easily identified, but to be useful it needs to be broken down into categories including development, operation, administration and teaching. The main reason for some separation of staff time is that operating costs will always be incurred whereas development is not a constant activity and its costs need to be treated differently.

Exact definitions, however, are not easy and individuals will always vary in their classifications. The share of overheads and services is a cost that is particularly open to different interpretation; some institutions will give costs, which they believe represent direct calls on their resources, while others will make an apportionment proportional to some other measure such as staff numbers.

Identification of outputs is generally more difficult because of the changing state of the educational environment. There is no possibility of keeping everything constant except the particular innovation: both students and staff come and go, the curriculum changes, and emphasis shifts from one area to another. As the new methods are usually only operating at the edge of the general educational activity, it is not possible to measure directly any change in the level or speed of learning. Many would argue that this is not in any case a desirable aim, as most innovations change the style and content of learning and not merely the mechanical process of acquiring knowledge, and therefore the previous measurements are no longer appropriate. There are exceptions to this, particularly in areas of training, where the skills to be learned can be specified in a much more precise manner than in education, and where an increased level or speed of attainment can be measured with some degree of objectivity. In general though, the principal outcome of educational change is something which cannot be subjected to the quantitative discipline of a financial analysis and which falls properly in the province of educational evaluation.

It is important nevertheless to identify the nature of the change being aimed at in different projects, so that this may be considered alongside the scale of resources involved. Some computer managed projects, for instance, involve the restructuring of the curriculum, teaching resources and learning styles and thus change the learning process for the student. In other projects, by contrast it is impossible for the student even to detect that a change has taken place, as the system is totally directed towards providing better information for the staff.

Finally, effects on student time may be identified. The number of students involved, both actually and potentially, is relevant as is some indication of their time involvement, perhaps measured as a percentage of total contact time. Although there are as many types of use as there are CAL projects and contact time is no direct measure of quality of learning, information of this type does serve to give some broad indication, when taken in conjunction with other data, of the possible impact of the change.

## 1.3 Measurement of change

### *1.3.1 When to measure*

The first question to be faced when setting out on a cost analysis of an innovative project is the definition of the period with which the analysis should be concerned. When does a 'project' start and when does it cease to be a project? In the early stages the level of activity (and hence the resource usage) is probably low, as perhaps only one person is considering the feasibility of the approach. Later the project gathers momentum (and usually staff) and a formal feasibility study might be followed by a development phase. This is the period in NDPCAL's projects when most of the systems and much of the educational development were undertaken, and it can take a long time before any tangible results occur. Eventually, the materials are tested and there might be a formal 'pilot trial', usually consisting of live running on a limited scale. As a result of this there could be more development work modifying the material in the light of the lessons learned, before full operational use commences. Typically, the level of activity might follow the pattern shown in the graph below

*Figure 1*

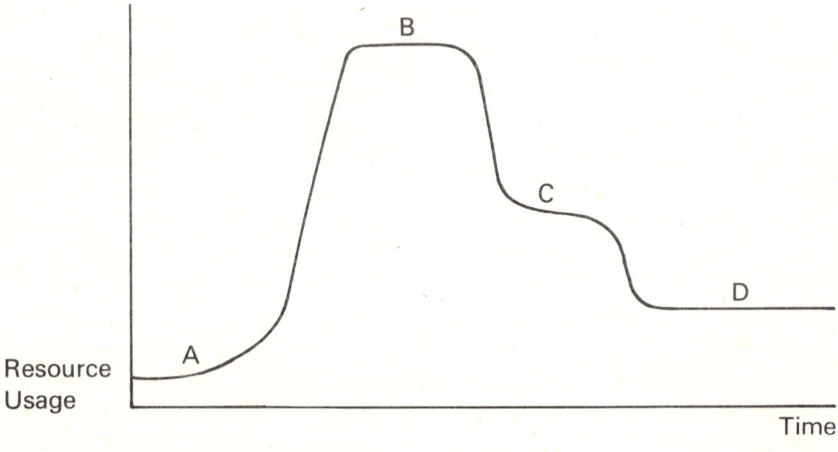


Roughly speaking, A represents the initial planning; B the feasibility study and development phase; C the pilot trial; and D the operational running stages. However, the breakdown is seldom as neat as this in

practice. Some pilot testing and even real operation of the first materials to be developed will often take place simultaneously with the development of other material, all activities making demands on the same resources in ways which interact with each other and often defy analysis. Again, even when a genuine operational phase is reached it will not normally mean an end to development as, if the system is successful, it will usually be extended to include other topics or different courses; this is true of virtually all the National Programme's projects which have only had a life that is very short in terms of educational change. It is difficult with this pattern of resource expenditure to know how to express the costs of a project in a useful way for a policy-maker who is looking for something expressed in pounds per year or per student. Other problems arise in certain projects at the two ends of the time scale. Some projects received significant investment before NDPCAL involvement, either out of internal resources or from other agencies and it is often difficult to obtain useful data for our own purposes. Other projects, particularly those in the military sector, started relatively late in the Programme and have not reached a stage at which any projections can be made into the steady state.

*1.3.2 Methods of measurement*

The main resources and outcomes to be identified have already been given in section 1.2, but the actual procedure of measurement presents problems of definition, data collection and interpretation.

The most costly resource in all projects is staff time. Where staff are specifically funded for a project, usually being specially recruited or seconded and made responsible for the detailed development work, the overall measurement of this cost is straightforward. When existing staff devote part of their time (which for example might otherwise have been spent on their personal research) the task is more difficult, as there is no ready-made system for recording their contribution to the project. Sometimes, staff may be working on aspects of reorganizing a course in connection with the project and part of their time may be spent in actively using the new material in teaching. Is this research, development, teaching or (in some cases where they may be teaching outside their normal environment) sales promotion? Even with staff working full-time on a project the problem of breaking down their time into categories is not always easy.

Computing facilities are another example of a cost area which provides problems unless the project has its own installation. If use is made of a central computer, how is this to be costed? Often there is no real cost as the project makes use of spare capacity or off-peak time. To neglect this entirely, however, would give a distorted picture to other potential users, where demands may have a real financial impact on their own installations, perhaps involving the purchase of new equipment. Even in the institution where the project was developed, costs may become significant in the future, once the sytsem becomes more widely accepted and used. There are ways of calculating hypothetical (and in some cases actual) charges that can be levied on projects, but there is no standard or ideal basis which best reflects the true long-term demand made on central computing facilities. Sometimes a project has a large 'share' in a minicomputer and the obvious procedure here is to divide the total cost approximately between the users on the basis of the processor time used. Even here the costing is artificial in that, if one project closes down, the computing bill will not be reduced in proportion to that project's nominal share of the total cost. In computing particularly, and in all costs to some extent, it is not possible to avoid the costs reflecting the purely fortuitous circumstances in which the individual projects find themselves, and this clearly introduces much random variation and consequent inaccuracy when attempting to generalize from particular applications.

With regard to the collection of cost data, a major problem of the financial evaluation was in finding the resources to carry out the work involved. It was obviously not possible with over 30 projects using the time budget of the financial evaluation, and the only alternative was to ask project managers to shoulder most of the burden. The obvious drawback to this approach is that it was impossible to define categories of cost precisely enough and different individuals inevitably made different interpretations. The problem would have been severe enough if all projects had been similar in their nature, but in the case of the National Programme it was compounded by the variety of types of applications, institutions and project organizations, so that absolute uniformity of data provision was not possible.

As far as measuring outcomes is concerned, the problem presented by the qualitative nature of most of the benefits has already been discussed. Some quantitative data can be collected relating to numbers of staff and students involved, estimates of terminal utilization, number of packages transferred to other users and the proportion of student contact time occupied by the new material. More difficult information to collect includes that on the reallocation of staff time or the attitudes of staff to the innovation; although such data are susceptible to quantitative measurement, the time involved in collecting it is prohibitive on all but a small scale in a few of the projects. In some cases however, useful views have been obtained from questionnaires and in others hard data have been provided on quantitative benefits including savings in staff time and equipment or sales of material to other institutions.

### *1.3.3 Units*

The choice of units in which to record resource usage was something which had to be decided early in the evaluation. There is a natural inclination in a financial evaluation to use monetary units from the start as final figures will need to be presented in this way. However, there were strong arguments in favour of using the units in which resource expenditure naturally occurs, such as man-days, seconds of computer processing time or square feet of accommodation. In a period of rapid inflation this allows the cost data to be easily updated in the future and 'inflation-proofs' the basic information.

A second, and probably more important reason, is that by collecting data in its basic form, options are kept open for different approaches in the later analysis. It is all too easy to convert everything to financial units and thereby lose sight of fundamental differences between resources. There is a world of difference to a finance officer between £1000 spent on capital equipment, £1000 which represents a contribution of the time of an existing member of staff and £1000 which is a notional share of the institution's overheads.

## 1.4 Analysis and presentation

There are three distinct problems in analysing costs for presentation in a summative report:

- how should the very different types of resource usage be combined to produce an overall cost
- how should the variation in costs over the life of the project be treated
- in what units should the results be presented (a separate issue from that of the units in which costs are collected); and are there other figures which can be used for comparison?

*1.4.1 Combining resource data*

Resources vary greatly in their degree of 'reality'. Some, such as the purchase of a dedicated computer, are easily identifiable and undeniably real; others, such as the time of academic staff, are much more difficult to isolate and are less discernible in their impact. Is this latter type of cost to be given its full financial weight as a national resource, treated as a clever way of obtaining development on the cheap, or is it perhaps to be thought of simply as part of the normal and legitimate activity of academics?

At one extreme we can produce a 'total cost' which combines the effects of all resources in monetary terms. This is certainly one useful method, as it gives the total resource contributions that can conceivably be included. But this approach is not the best one for all purposes, as it includes elements which, it could be argued, are not true costs. Expenditure on capital equipment or on the salaries of specially recruited staff are the most indisputably real in that if the project had not taken place these costs would not have been incurred. But other items such as the time of existing staff are in a different category, since their use on the project has not affected the institution's cash flow; yet these items nevertheless attract an economic cost, if not a financial one, in that the project work has displaced other activity and can thus be said to bear an opportunity cost. There are other 'costs' such as the allocation of a share of the institution's overheads which, at least in the short term and in some applications, are purely notional and where the existence of the project has had no discernible effect whatever.

A purely marginal financial cost represents the other extreme from a total cost, as this includes only those items through which a project directly affects the cash position of an institution or authority. However, enough has been said to demonstrate that there can be a bewildering variety of choice of costs: total, marginal, financial or economic. The best approach in individual cases must depend on the particular circumstances and, although it is possible to adopt a basic methodological approach (see Chapter 2 of this report; Fielden, 1978a; and Fielden and Pearson, 1978) no hard and fast rules can be given.

*1.4.2 Treatment of variation over time*

The likely pattern of resource usage over the life of a project has already been discussed (see Figure 1). Decisions are often made in practice by considering only the last part of this cost curve on the grounds that the past cost is 'sunk' and only running costs are relevant to decisions about the future. This is fallacious on two grounds: firstly, development costs will be important in any wider application of the innovation outside its existing environment; and secondly, development is not merely a once-for-all investment, as educational material and system's software become outdated and will eventually need to be replaced.

It is necessary therefore to isolate development costs from the other activities of the project and some of the problems of definition have already been discussed above. Even where the cost of the development phase can be separated out, it will normally include a range of different activities such as systems development, educational development, administrative tasks, teaching with experimental material and promotion. Some of the work not directly concerned with development, but forming part of the development phase (in particular the often large amount of administration) will be necessary even in the steady state; but much of it will have occurred primarily because of the abnormal development activity with its necessary tasks of reporting to departmental and institutional committees, and to NDPCAL, and in providing information for the independent evaluations. How much of this type of activity to attribute to development proper and how much to write off as a once-for-all cost is something that can only be subjectively judged on an individual project basis.

When an estimate of development cost has been made, it must be combined in some way with the running costs to give an overall figure. Ideally, we should aim at deriving a 'steady state' cost which expresses the annual cost of running an application of a given type and size. It should somehow incorporate both development and operating costs in such a way that it expresses the 'average' cost in long-term, although in any one year the actual cost might be expected to be higher or lower than the 'steady state' cost.

*1.4.3 Unit costs and comparisons*

Unit costs are those in the form of a ratio such as pounds per student or pounds per student-hour, as opposed to a simple statement of costs in pounds, eg, a project cost £50,000. Cost per student-hour is generally considered as an appropriate measure for CAL, but there can be problems of definition where more than one student uses each computer terminal and here cost per student-terminal-hour might be more appropriate. Where CAL packages are used for group demonstration, say in the middle of an otherwise conventional lecture, unit costs would not be very helpful and have not been calculated. Some projects use the computer as a data base to answer requests from students for information on certain topics and here a cost per inquiry seems the most appropriate measure, although it is a unit that is difficult to relate to any other known costs and thus has only limited value.

With CML an annual cost per student seems the best unit cost, although care should be taken in using it, as it is a measure which is independent of the proportion of the curriculum that is covered by the CML system: projects vary a great deal in this respect from those which computer manage the whole course to those dealing with part of one subject area for a few hours.

Finally, in order for costs of new methods to be meaningful they need to be related in some way to those of conventional methods. Here again there are difficulties as the value of an hour's CAL tuition is not to be equated with that of an hour of a conventional lecture, tutorial or practical session; indeed, a main aim of CAL is often to provide an entirely new way of mastering certain concepts or to do things which could not be achieved by any other means. It can therefore be objected that a direct comparison of CAL and conventional costs is invidious or at least naïve. Nevertheless, without some comparison the policy-maker has no framework at all within which to evaluate the resource implications of the new methods and in the end he must be trusted to take into account the different quality of innovative applications in making his own value judgements.

## 1.5 Audiences

One of the most important findings to come out of the early stages of the evaluation was the realization how greatly the perceptions of different policy-makers varied with regard to the importance of various cost elements. In general, three levels of decision-making can be identified: the department, the institution and the nation. It is possible, when dealing with individual projects, to derive separate costs for each level which can be different from one another. It is also possible because of these different viewpoints for decisions to be made without realization of the full resource implications at the other levels.

At the departmental level the only items which concern the head of the department (or school in a local authority project) are those which must be paid for out of the departmental budget, or which make demands on the time of his staff or other resources; he is not generally concerned with, for example, the use of central computing facilities unless the cost of these is charged out. At the institutional (or local authority) level a decision-maker will be concerned with the provision of any facilities which might affect his budget or make competing demands on limited resources, and central facilities, services and accommodation enter the calculations at this level. He will not however be generally interested in the time spent by the staff of particular departments since this has no effect on his institutional budget, nor will he be greatly influenced by the cost of specially recruited development staff, provided these are funded by an outside agency such as the National Programme. It is only at the national level that all costs, financial or economic, irrespective of their source or effect can be fully taken into account.

While it is the national costs which are the most relevant ones in judging the real value of innovation, the others cannot be neglected as it is they which often determine the decision-making process at other levels and hence influence the long-term acceptance of new methods. Recognition of these different levels can however make the presentation of information at the individual project level a complex procedure and there is a danger of providing too many sub-sets of costs which confuse the main issue.

## 1.6 Technical cost issues

### *1.6.1 Development costs*

We have already discussed the problems encountered in estimating development costs, but not the technical one of how the cost should be treated when it has been established.

Conservative accounting practice suggests that development costs which recur on a regular basis ought not to be capitalized at all and should be written off in the year in which they are incurred. This approach might be sensible in, say, a manufacturing industry where development is not a major cost, but it makes little sense where the development costs of a project dwarf its annual running costs. Jamison, Klees and Wells (1976) have proposed the concept of average costs during the years of a project's development and operation. They suggest the study should predict the development and running costs which remain each year in, say, a ten-year projection, and then derive an average cost for each year. According to the time-scale when the study is undertaken the average cost will fall as time progresses. This approach, while perhaps making economic sense, has the disadvantage of not leading to a simple annual cost, which can be thought of as the 'steady-state' cost of the project. Although there is no standard answer to this problem, it is probably most sensible in the case of CAL projects to attempt to identify the point at which the project reaches a steady state and to treat the development costs up to that point as an asset to be depreciated in the same way as a piece of machinery over its expected life. In some cases most of the expenditure up to the steady-state stage might be treated in this way. In others there might be a disproportionate amount of administration (eg, due to the multi-institutional nature of the development) or costs that could properly be described as operational, due to the development being particularly protracted; these must obviously be allowed for in calculating the development cost to be depreciated.

### *1.6.2 Capital costs*

Conventional educational cost accounting practice is to treat capital as a 'sunk cost'; but it is more realistic, as with development costs, to treat it for our purposes as a depreciating asset. A more difficult decision is whether to use historic costs or replacement costs in the depreciation calculation. This is particularly difficult in the case of computing equipment, where predicting a replacement cost implies a knowledge of the future state of a rapidly developing technology.

Finally, should the opportunity costs of capital be considered, since education receives resources which might be invested elsewhere by the Government? If so, what rate of interest should be used? On the whole practical arguments dominate this issue: as such a charge would always be debatable in educational circles, and would probably confuse the main points, it seems best to ignore this extra complication.

## 1.7 Conclusions

The main effort of the financial evaluation during the course of the National Programme has gone into the evaluation of the separate projects. In most cases detailed reports were prepared on them for the Programme Committee when it considered further funding at the mid-term evaluation stage. This chapter has discussed the main problems encountered in that work and has also indicated the way our own preferences have influenced the choice of data and its treatment.

In this report little cost data of the detailed type discussed is given on individual projects. This is because such a mass of data would be out of place in a summative report and, in any case, would need to be so heavily qualified that it would make very difficult reading. The presentation of the problems, however, will, we hope, be of help to others carrying out similar work in the future.

# 2. Methodology of the evaluation

## 2.1 Role and objectives

A simple description of the purpose of the financial evaluation would be that it was to answer all questions on the resources or costs involved in innovations sponsored by NDPCAL. In an early paper (Fielden, 1974) this was elaborated when three main objectives were defined:

'— to identify fully the resource implications of each project
— to produce reliable estimates for each project of the cost of broader implementation and assimilation of the development in other institutions
— to assist project directors in establishing information systems and in assessing financial options'.

These objectives have been maintained throughout the evaluation. As we have seen in Chapter 1, however, there are many problems in putting financial labels on educational activities. Thus, the second objective has involved a considerable amount of definition and clarification of costs and audiences, as well as the continuing problem of identifying the change in a dynamic environment.

## 2.2 Initial stages

The National Programme commissioned 35 projects which by the end of 1977 involved, Hooper suggests, 690 teaching staff in 47 institutions. More than 100 other teaching institutions had also received packages, or CAL material, from those staff directly funded by NDPCAL (Hooper, 1977). The scale of NDPCAL's activities was thus substantial. The financial evaluation had only limited resources, namely 112 man-weeks spread over five years, with which to carry out its task. That this was achieved was due to two factors. Firstly, in the early days of the Programme, John Fielden was able to ensure that NDPCAL's own procedures on regular reporting and submission of information to the Directorate were compatible with the requirements of the financial evaluation; and secondly, we were able to persuade directors of the individual projects to maintain records themselves of information which would be needed for the evaluation. Had the financial evaluation not been appointed at an early stage and had it not been asked by Hooper to give advice on administrative procedures, this fortunate situation would not have arisen.

The early months of the evaluation involved visits to new projects as soon as they were approved in order to meet the director and help him or her devise appropriate information collection systems. Although some guidelines were produced (see Appendix D) on the data and questions which it was hoped all projects would tackle, it was not always reasonable to expect projects to follow them. Directors were given discretion in designing their own methods of obtaining data on staff time and were urged to give priority to computerized record keeping of student numbers and terminal use. The task was challenging: to try to ensure that thirty different institutions with very different atmospheres and procedures adhered voluntarily to a common discipline. Inevitably, there were one or two who gave low priority to the financial evaluation and who devised their own short cuts to providing the data. The great majority allowed themselves to be persuaded of the need to help and ensured that their staff cooperated with all the requirements. We cannot say what contributed to this happy state of affairs, whether it was the eagerness to play the game with a well-endowed funding agency or the inherent reasonableness of the requests.

The evaluation had to undertake a certain amount of in-service training on financial definitions and procedures. Talks were given to three meetings of new project staff and a paper was presented to a conference in spring 1974. In addition, explanatory notes were written for applicants to NDPCAL on how to treat inflation in budget preparation and on the group purchasing scheme which had been devised for terminals. NDPCAL's formal procedures for project application gave considerable emphasis to information on resources and finance. One unusual requirement, which possibly symbolized the awareness of costs, was that projects had to define their financial objectives as part of this formal application. Directors were somewhat bemused by this requirement, but many made a good try. Some were extremely precise and probably lived to regret it, three inflationary years later.

Among the objectives defined by projects were:

— to ensure the ongoing project is viable; a quoted £4.35 per student-year at 1974 prices (with 4000 students using the system) is the target' (Hertfordshire Computer Managed Mathematics Project)
— to determine the scale of the CAL operation and the nature of the

computing facilities necessary to bring the costs to a level acceptable to the institutions involved, probably an average overall cost of about £2.00 per student-hour' (CALCHEM Project; see Appendix C).

There is no doubt that the early statement of these objectives forced directors to think ahead in terms of student numbers and costs and showed some of them the crucial significance of scale. The existence of the forecasts also gave added zest to the recalculations of cost at the mid-term evaluation and final review sessions.

### 2.3 Information requirements

The data collection in the National Programme has been substantial. Some projects have complained of its bulk and of the time and effort it involved. There have, however, been subsidiary benefits to the projects. As a result of their initial energies they had ready answers to questions and well polished material for external audiences. As queries increasingly came to revolve round cost and resources, they were well prepared. One project gave a display at the annual gathering of academics in the same discipline. The most common question inquirers asked was 'What does it cost?'

#### *2.3.1 Staff time*

The National Programme spent about £1,650,000 on people and an unexpectedly small sum, £402,000 (equivalent to 16% of its budget) on equipment. It was clearly crucial to find out how NDPCAL-funded staff spent their time and also to glean as much as possible about how existing academic staff used the time they devoted to the projects. The crucial distinction in the use of time was between development time and operational time; that is, effort which would have a long-term benefit and effort which would help only the year in question. Accordingly, project directors were asked to ensure that NDPCAL-funded staff maintained records of their effort split between:

- technical computer-oriented development work on hardware, software or coding
- educational development devoted to the design of teaching material and handouts and the incorporation of the computer based packages into the curriculum
- operational or teaching time with students

— administration, travelling, conferences, etc.

While it was reasonable to expect NDPCAL-funded staff to keep records in some detail, project directors had to approach academic staff very delicately with their request. Some asked for an estimate each term in whatever units (eg hours, man-days or percentage of time) the individual cared to give, while one asked participants to complete a monthly time-sheet. Predictably, staff found this latter approach uncongenial and after a period it was modified to a termly questionnaire. Some projects decided for their own purposes to introduce further sub-categories of time such as internal evaluation and time spent on transfers of material to other institutions. In Appendix D2 we describe how several projects tackled the time allocation issue.

As a result of the high degree of cooperation with this key data request, projects were able to provide a great amount of information on their expenditure of effort at the evaluation meeting. CALCHEM, for example, could give a detailed breakdown of the 1.5 academic man-years spent on the project in 1976/77. This showed what a large proportion of effort went on administration. The detailed analysis was:

| | |
|---|---|
| Systems and program development | 0.24 man-years |
| Curriculum development | 0.26 man-years |
| Extra supervision/teaching | 0.09 man-years |
| Publicity and dissemination | 0.59 man-years |
| Administration | 0.37 man-years |

Although there was only one project where academics preferred not to cooperate at all, it became clear during the course of the evaluation that many staff were somewhat arbitrary in their time allocations. For this reason it is dangerous to place too much reliance on the accuracy of such time data, and it should be used only to identify broad themes.

*2.3.2 Computer time*

A second important resource for all projects was computer time. The users of hardware fell into three categories: those with their own faculty or departmental minicomputer dedicated to the project, those enjoying time on a central institutional computer service which had no formal charging system, and those unfortunate few who were buying time from an external bureau service. The first category gave little difficulty as the total costs of the computer would fall on the project and the main concern related to statistics of use which often required special control programs to be written. With the second category came the greatest data problems. The programs developed by projects rarely took more than one per cent of the main central processor's (CPU) time; the storage space they required on disc was a little more substantial and on occasions they demanded all the on-line terminals. Indeed, they were often the largest user of the central terminal room. How would one bring together all these different resource impacts into one measure? Was there one algorithm which would show a project's computer demand? If there was a local formula, would it not be based on the institution's own configuration and prove useless elsewhere? These difficulties are well-known and the evaluation had to admit that it was in a weak position to ask for any special data collection. Attention was thus focused on approximate guesses of time used in the central processor, data on program size and specific information on terminal hours. The last category of user, customers of bureaux, tended to receive precise data on usage together with a specific charging algorithm which the regional centre or bureau adopted. This usually gave enough information. Fortunately, by the end of NDPCAL's life, no project was reliant on an external bureau and all had their dedicated mini or thoroughly compliant central computer service.

*2.3.3 Other direct costs*

Financial implications of the projects were, as regards direct costs, well covered by NDPCAL's financial reporting systems which required four-monthly statements (we had recommended this unusual time scale to help cut down administrative costs and to enable reconciliation with both central and local government accounting periods) with details of costs. Clearly this system omitted any costs which were met by the local authority or institution. As NDPCAL progressed towards its inevitable demise, it was Hooper's policy to ensure that the 'matched funding' element (the institutions' or authorities' contributions to the projects) grew in size, while NDPCAL's share decreased. Thus, in the Leeds Statistics Project, for example, the three participating institutions in 1976-77 took over the cost of maintaining the computer and the terminals from the Programme. The evaluation did its best to identify all the hidden costs of projects by using cost questionnaires (see Appendix D4) as the basis for calculating the notional future total cost of each of the projects. These, together with the reports required on matched funding, were, it was hoped, adequate to reveal the full direct cost implications.

*2.3.4 Indirect costs*

The projects had some indirect resource implications which were not always easy to identify. The checklist submitted to directors in 1974 (Appendix D1) raised some of these:

— effect on examination costs, book purchases, library budgets
— effect on technical officers' time, if laboratory experiments were replaced
— demands on academic staff outside the project who might have to learn about it in order to modify their own lectures or material.

Although these were given attention at the outset, it was found in the end that there were no cases where these costs were significant.

*2.3.5 Space*

Project directors were surprised to find themselves measuring their offices and terminal rooms in order to give NDPCAL information. In some cases it could be a material barrier to a transfer to find that the adoption of an innovation required 250 square feet of dedicated space. The collection of the space use as an item of data reflected the University Grants Committee's own concern with space utilization and capacity and enabled the total cost calculations of rental to be soundly based. The data allows us to make interesting comparisons. At the University of Surrey's CPTL Project, for example, the terminal room of 650 square feet provides 5500 student hours of instruction, while the existing experimental teaching laboratories of 4800 square feet give 12,000 hours of student use per annum. In the terminal room the annual depreciation charge on the equipment used is £6700, while in the laboratory it is virtually identical at £6300.

*2.3.6 Quantifiable outcomes*

These could be among the following types.

— Some measure of instruction provided, whether in student-terminal-hours, packages available, inquiries made or hours available: in Chapter 1 we have referred to some of the difficulties of selecting measures and it was clear that the evaluation had to be pragmatic in its choice. As a result no standard measure was possible. It proved surprisingly difficult to persuade all projects to record accurate data on terminal use, as in many cases special computer programs had to be written and manual logging-in systems never proved to be reliable. However, by the end of 1977 almost all projects were able to report reasonably accurate figures for the 1976/77 academic year. Some problems still remained: type of use could not always be identified, so that one was unable to say precisely how much time had been on 'free access' or revision by students; computer-based logging systems failed to record how many students were sitting round the terminal.

— Reduction in time or other resources devoted to instruction: the claims for saving in time, which we examine in greater detail later, were clearly important. At the New University of Ulster, for example, it is suggested that the use of the computer to manage an individualized learning course has led to a huge reduction in staff time devoted to marking. The Royal Signals Trade Training School hope that the use of the computer for course management will help them to reduce clerical staff. These are significant outcomes and were the focus for critical attention. Evidence of reduction in cash resources was also sought, but few claims were made.

— Tangible outcomes which are harder to quantify include more information on students (a feature of many CML projects), speedier instruction, because one hour at a terminal is more effective in terms of individual learning than one hour at a lecture, and (a concomitant benefit) an expanded syllabus which may have a closer link to recent research advances. Since the educational evaluation was looking in depth at claims of this kind, these outcomes were not pursued, as they involved qualitative factors outside our experience.

### 2.4 The principal work of the financial evaluation

The missionary phase of the financial evaluation was concentrated principally in the first year-and-a-half from May 1973 to December 1974. By that time 25 projects had been established. This was not the final total, as by 1977 a further 10 had been started. There was therefore a continuing need to visit new project directors and to help them establish data collection systems. The main effort of the evaluation however switched to analysis and reporting.

One of Hooper's major innovations was his emphasis on step-funding of projects with a mid-term evaluation meeting, as the key decision point about continuation (see Chapter 3). These meetings which began in the spring of 1975 were attended by the financial evaluators. It was necessary for us to have a preliminary meeting with the project director to review the information collected to date and to suggest how it might be presented to the external evaluators. Twenty-one evaluation meetings were held, mostly two days long. During them the project director took a day, often with copious documentation as well as audio-visual aids, to describe what the project had achieved. The second day was devoted to future plans and the inevitable request for further funding; it concluded with a private discussion among the evaluation team. The role of the financial evaluators was to raise resource issues, if the project director did not cover them, and to prepare a report on them for Programme Committee. The final decision on the progress of each project lay with the Committee and it had before it on each occasion a short report by the Programme Director, a slightly larger one by the financial evaluators and an even larger report by the educational evaluation team. All the evaluators were in attendance at the Programme Committee meeting.

Twenty-one financial evaluation reports were produced as a result of the mid-term evaluations. None has been published as they were confidential to the Committee. Although projects varied greatly in scope and function, the reports tried to follow a common framework. This had the following elements:

- a summary of achievements so far, giving quantitative data where possible
- a statement of resources spent compared with the budget
- a review of achievements compared with the financial objectives stated in the project proposal
- calculations of the marginal and total costs of the project from various viewpoints
- conclusions with cost projections for a 'hypothetical steady state' when the development activity had levelled off.

All the financial evaluation reports were agreed with project directors before they were submitted to the Committee. In some instances they were more influential in the project than anticipated. One project Steering Committee was so horrified by the unit cost figures emerging that it gave stronger emphasis to maximizing student numbers and to bringing in more participating institutions.

When projects entered their second stages, the evaluation was concerned to ensure that their data collection continued. Project directors were reminded of the need for it and various problems were drawn to their attention (Appendix D3). Throughout this period we continued to visit projects to keep abreast of any new developments.

Other work of the financial evaluation was less predictable; it included participation at national conferences, presentations at projects' own internal seminars and special visits to projects with resource difficulties or technical queries on costing.

In spring 1977 the pace hotted up. Richard Hooper had decided to ask projects to give a one-day final review presentation to a small evaluation team. The rationale was to enable him and the evaluators to have a 'data base', on which their generalizations should be based. Unless the projects provided information up to the end of the 1977 spring term, the *Final Report* from NDPCAL would not meet its printer's deadline. Without the incentive of further funding the final review meetings were less tense and project directors could join the team in objective reflections on their work and its future. The financial aspects were fully covered in one of the day's three sessions. As a preliminary to this, a checklist of issues had been sent to all projects with a cost calculation sheet, where relevant, to help some projects work out their total cost (see Appendix D4 for both documents). The 13 projects which held final evaluation meetings in the first half of 1977 were mostly those that had started earlier in the life of NPDCAL. During October and November 1977 the late starters, notably the military projects, held their final review sessions. Since the CAL and higher education projects predominated among the first 13, there is an inevitable bias in some of our conclusions towards the perspectives and problems of the tertiary sector. It is unfortunate that more of the industrial training and military projects were not initiated earlier in the five-year period.

What has been the product of this evaluation effort? We believe there are three main outcomes:

— a better understanding of the problems of micro-costing and a methodology that might have relevance elsewhere in education
— an appreciation, among project staff at least, of the importance of resource and financial considerations and a greater awareness of the practical problems of assessing and measuring them
— a body of published data on CAL and CML which will help

practitioners and outsiders in making decisions on future investment. This report has this as one of its aims. Later chapters include information on many practical aspects of CAL and CML, such as terminal usage and timetabling, program development times and the scope for realizable economies.

## 2.5 Measuring costs

### *2.5.1 Methodology*

In Chapter 1 we identified some of the problems concerning the costing of CAL and CML. These are also covered elsewhere in the broader context (Fielden, 1978) of all educational activities.

We considered the possible costing methods that could be adopted in the light of NDPCAL's time scale, the likely development curve of projects and the possible audiences for cost information. It was obvious that there was no point in calculating the costs of the projects while they were still developing. The only date which seemed realistic was 1977/78, after NDPCAL funding had ceased, when the institution itself had taken over the financial burdens. All costings were based on this hypothetical future steady state although for many projects it involved crystal gazing and some brave assumptions about institutional support.

It was clear that the three levels of audience, which were identified in Chapter 1, were interested in different information. The national level would understand national total costs to facilitate comparisons between projects and with conventional activities; the institutional and departmental levels would be much more interested in marginal costs expressed in the basic units which made sense at local levels of decision-making. The information systems existed to meet these needs and it was now a question of analysing and aggregating the data. The marginal cost levels presented fewer technical problems as more of the data remained in its basic unit. A definition difficulty arose. What does marginal cost mean when staff are tenured and cannot be dismissed? Is one-third of a man's time a marginal cost? A definition of marginal as that which can be saved or avoided, was therefore chosen. Where a project is sharing part of a computer and then winds up, there is no saving, as the computer will still operate, but with a greater slack. The fraction of its maintenance and depreciation costs will fall on other users.

The principal technical problems arise in the calculation of total cost. The cost calculation sheet already referred to in Appendix D4 showed how these issues were answered. The costing was divided into three parts: capital costs, operating costs and development costs, and these were then combined to give the steady state annual cost.

### *2.5.2 Capital costs*

The capital cost calculation relates to projects which either have their own minicomputer or use a central service. Depreciation is calculated on the historic cost assuming a seven-year life. In the late 1960s it was assumed that computer costs would fall rapidly; this has not happened and prices have kept pace with inflation. Specifications and capabilities have improved so that the same amount of real money buys greater power and greater storage. Because of this and because the accountancy profession is still far from unanimous about methods of using replacement costs, the historic cost basis has been used for the depreciation calculation. In the similar calculation for terminals the historic cost figure has also been taken, but has been depreciated over five years. Predictions as regards terminals have proved equally awry. At the start of the National Programme there were gloomy comments about projects basing themselves too heavily on out-of-date technology, but the day of the cheap interactive graphics terminal (with selective erase facility) steadfastly did not dawn in 1973/77. Their costs have climbed to match inflation so that a Tektronix 4010-1 terminal which cost £2030 in January 1973 cost £4076 (excluding VAT and import duty) in January 1977. At least, however, cheaper improved graphics are becoming available (Shirley, 1977). Included in the capital cost element of the total cost calculation in Appendix D4 are maintenance costs for all hardware and any space or labour costs related to the computer or terminal rooms.

### *2.5.3 Operating cost*

The calculation of operating cost is generally uncontentious. As one might expect, it contains the direct costs attached to the project including academic time supervising and operating the materials. Within this head will be a small element of continuing development activity, as CAL material or CML systems are amended and improved. Also included are consumable costs, an imputed rental for the space used, telephone and modem charges and an estimate of institutional overheads related to the activity.

*2.5.4 Development costs*

In Chapter 1 some approaches to treating development cost have been outlined. The evaluation has chosen an approach which is novel in education, but has precedents in industry. The relatively small amount of development which continues after the steady state has been reached has been included in the operating cost, as mentioned above, as there seems no reason for treating this any differently from other recurrent expenditure. However, the heavy development investment of academic and technical staff in the earlier phases of the projects (identified through their time analyses) is an investment which benefits the future. As it usually exceeds by a considerable margin the normal investment which a department would expect to give to developing an element in a course, it should be separately identified. We chose to treat development expenditure in the same way as a capital asset and write it off over a number of years. But what is the life of a package or a course? Here, any guess could be proved wrong, so an arbitrary life of five years was selected. During the initial stages of the evaluation it was hoped to separate technical development costs with a life of seven years equal to the computer depreciation period from educational development costs with a five-year benefit. The complexities of this proved too great and a five-year write-off period was applied to all development.

Development costs were assumed to be all the project expenditure which did not benefit or relate to the year in which it arose. Thus the trial operation, and in later years the normal teaching use, of materials were excluded from development. Administration costs were also left out. There were two ways of calculating development cost; the careful build-up from time records of development activity, and the short-cut shown in Part C of the cost calculation sheet in Appendix D4. In this latter method the total costs were ascertained and capital costs were deducted; an estimate in percentage terms (based on time records) was then made of non-development activity. This was then subtracted from the net total cost figure. The resulting development cost was divided by five to arrive at an annual charge.

The approach to calculating development cost is an arbitrary one and has made some sensitive assumptions. It would be difficult to avoid these failings. The evaluation felt that the developmental element in costings was so important that it needed separate attention. We find for example that in three higher education projects it exceeds 45% of the total cost, while in seven it represents between 28% and 38%. In some it amounted to five times the annual operating costs. The combination of these global figures and individual data on package development times leads one to question the absence of a mechanism of investment appraisal in higher education. Is there any way we can build in some check mechanisms, so that this time investment is matched against its expectations and likely outcomes? Is it not right to think a little more of accountability where development effort is concerned? Although much research is not suitable for such rigorous scrutiny, should development costs also escape?

### *2.5.5 Factors omitted*

The addition of the three cost categories produces a total cost. Some cost elements which are often found in other similar costing exercises have been omitted. These came from economics rather than accountancy. They are as follows.

— Interest on capital employed: although no other published British educational cost analysis has included this element, it should properly appear so as to reflect the government's decision to invest resources in education rather than other activities. As the National Programme's funding was a marginal activity in the sense that it could have been stopped at any time, this cost element is particularly relevant. Two arguments overruled this; so much of NDPCAL's funding was on people and the concept of this earning interest seems unrealistic; also the choice of interest rate is always arbitrary and would inevitably cause debate.

— Discount factors to reflect the time element in expenditure and the delay before benefits arise are a standard feature of industrial project appraisals. The stream of net benefits is discounted to a net present value using the current market interest rate being paid for loans. The project is then seen to have a positive or a negative rate of return. This approach was not adopted for the principal reason, as we have seen, that there are almost no measurable benefits to set against the cost. Nor is government accustomed in education to long-term appraisals of projections of expenditure other than through the framework of the PESC (Public Expenditure Survey Committee) system, the details of which are not publicly revealed.

— The third factor consciously omitted was earnings foregone, as it was irrelevant to any of the possible decisions on CAL or CML.

*2.5.6 Difficulties in comparing projects*

As a result of the cost methodology adopted, answers can now be given to the three levels of inquirers about the projects. Each receives information that suits his requirements in different units and with a different cost definition (marginal or total). Two examples of these sets of answers are given in the project case studies in Appendices A and B. In this respect the methodology has been successful. Where it has failed is in finding any cost measure which can be used for comparative purposes. As soon as one studies an individual project's cost profile in depth a large number of special factors emerge. These will cover issues such as:

— the skill of the individuals concerned, their willingness to adopt long hours in their enthusiasm for the project
— their relationship with other staff and ability to win cooperation from them in using CAL materials
— the role of CAL and the complexity and size of materials produced
— the choice of subject for CAL since esoteric, peripheral or core topics will have different potential markets
— the energy devoted to promoting transfers elsewhere
— the absence of reliable data on use made elsewhere of any ideas or materials transferred; to this extent the project's student hours or measures of outcome will be understated
— the career ambitions of staff, their research interests and plans for movement to other institutions
— idiosyncracies of hardware provision will have influenced costs and the attitude of students and staff to CAL. (An initial history of computer breakdowns may take a period to overcome).

Factors such as these will have affected the total cost of the project and its cost per student-hour. If the costs of two projects were to be compared, full account should be taken of the effect of these factors in both cases. In addition major conceptual problems arise with the educational outcome. A student-hour on one CAL package will have a different educational 'value' from an hour on another. Even if we are able to agree and apply a typology of learning such as UNCAL has expounded (Kemmis, 1976), we are no nearer to knowing whether learning at level A should cost twice or four times as much as learning at level B.

Therefore the evaluation has been reluctant to compare costs per pupil or student-hour between projects. Absolute and total costs have been quoted, as they have relevance to outside inquirers who might wish to invest in similar activities, but we have avoided citing Project A as the 'best' because its cost appears as £3 an hour compared with Project B at £20 an hour. Unit costs are too easily quoted without the very long string of assumptions and qualifications that should accompany them.

### 2.6 Criticisms of the evaluation

The role of the financial evaluation has sometimes been misunderstood by project staff or visitors to NDPCAL. Although constantly referred to as the 'auditors' or the 'money men', we have sought to avoid the cost accounting image and to don the unique mantle of resource evaluator. Cost calculations, for the reasons given in the previous section, were not seen as the major outcome of our work and we preferred to concentrate on non-monetary units and to talk about resource implications of change. We believe this role has been valuable in influencing attitudes to expenditure in projects. Clearly however there has been little need to preach broad financial awareness to many staff in view of the dismal economic situation both inside and outside educational institutions. We may have been of use in specific project circumstances and in encouraging directors to adopt policies which maximize student-hours.

During the four-and-a-half years of the evaluation our work has not received much critical attention, either favourable or otherwise. Recently some critical comments have been made which we consider here, because they have revelance to other future evaluation studies of this kind.

Hooper wrote in his *Final Report* that 'both evaluation agencies had difficulties keeping up with the size and the pace of the Programme'. This is true and the lesson for the future relates to the size and scale of evaluation effort. Appendix E shows a detailed analysis of the 112 man-weeks which were devoted to the financial evaluation of 35 projects. There is no doubt that we underestimated the manpower needed in the time budgets established in May 1973 and June 1975. Not only did the National Programme have more projects than anticipated, but they each had many participating institutions. Initial budgets which were based on one day's visit to one project were absurdly wrong with CALCHEM or the Engineering Sciences Project with their nine and six institutions respectively. NDPCAL was also very active in promoting internal meetings and seminars and in making external presentations and conferences. Attendance at these, although not essential, was a valuable way of meeting several project directors. As a result of these time pressures, the projects established last (those in the military and industrial sectors) received less attention than the earliest projects. They were not visited so often, as their work was not usually at an advanced enough stage to justify worthwhile predictions of the future steady-state costs. We suggest that a workable norm for future financial evaluations would be a time allocation of between four and six man-weeks per project depending on its complexity and state of development. This should enable detailed reports to be produced of the kind in Appendices A and B.

Other criticisms related to the techniques used. One project director thought the approach to evaluation was simplistic and naïve in its identification of benefits. He considered that staff and students gained many advantages from involvement in a CAL/CML project which should be taken into account by the financial evaluation; simply stopping at the number of hours of instruction provided was not enough, he suggested. We entirely accept his point, but consider that almost all the aspects he identified are outside the remit of the financial evaluation and should more properly be covered by the educational evaluation. One specific criticism was levelled at our methodology for calculating development costs. This has been fully explained in Chapter 1 and section 5 of this chapter. We acknowledge that our method is unusual, but are prepared to defend it in the context of the innovation concerned and the scale of the funds spent on development activities.

## 2.7 Conclusion

In this chapter and in Appendix D we have gone into some detail about our work and its methodology. In June 1973 *The Times Educational Supplement* hailed the appointment of external evaluators at the start of NDPCAL's life as 'a contrast with the conventional wisdom approach of the Schools Council' and suggested that a comparative study of the two evaluation approaches could be valuable. We have aimed to provide some of the evidence for such a study.

Although the product of the evaluation was popularly supposed to be lists of unit costs, we have concentrated on statements about resources and measures of space, time and terminal use. We are aware of all the limitations of unit cost calculations and therefore use them sparingly. In those cases where they are relevant we have calculated comparative and relative costs. We hope that one of the major outcomes of our work will be a greater understanding of the value and limitations of cost studies in education.

# 3. The management of NDPCAL

## 3.1 Introduction

The managerial ethos with its prespecified targets, measurable outputs and firm budgetary control procedures, is traditionally assumed by academic staff to be wholly inappropriate to the world of research and development. Richard Hooper has claimed that the Directorate adopted novel approaches in the management of the Programme (Hooper, 1978) and has stressed the managerial content of these innovations. In this chapter we shall scrutinize these claims, examine how the innovations worked in practice and consider finally whether they could be applied elsewhere. This chapter is based on correspondence and interviews with the Directorate and project directors on the subject of NDPCAL's management style and procedures.

## 3.2 The context of NDPCAL

NDPCAL was a rarity in educational funding for several reasons.

— It had a predetermined life, which was short in the context of projects of the type involved. Ignoring the time the preliminary grant applications took to be approved and the inevitable tailing-off period in the last year as project staff sought other employment, the maximum productive period for a project was four years. Thus, the tight timetable was a continual constraint.

— Its emphasis was firmly fixed on development rather than research. The Directorate was forced to blur the distinction at times, since not enough preliminary research in CAL had been carried out to justify a portfolio solely of development projects. As a result a feasibility study category was devised for projects in relatively uncharted areas.

— The size of projects was larger than with other educational funding bodies. The 35 projects received an average sum of over £70,000, compared with the SSRC's £16,000 for the 51 projects financed by the Educational Research Board in the two years 1974/76. Although it could be argued that this was a Directorate decision, it must also be pointed out that it is very unlikely that two or three times the number of NDPCAL projects could have been found.

— The subject matter was homogeneous in the technical sense to the extent that all projects faced common problems; there was thus a cohesiveness to the portfolio and individual project directors found it easy to have a sense of community with each other.

These factors had a significance to the Director when he began to plan the management of the Programme. The one-off nature of the exercise freed him from some traditional practices of funding agencies, the development bias meant that he could, if he wished, ask for more rigid monitoring than usual, the tight timetable gave a real sense of urgency and led almost inevitably to an emphasis on project management skills, while the small number of projects would allow the Directorate to get to know projects well, if they so desired.

### 3.3 The new approaches

Richard Hooper in 'Some new approaches to research and development funding' (Hooper, 1978) has outlined the ways in which NDPCAL managed its projects. He is modest about the novelty of the approaches and claims only that NDPCAL is 'the first funding agency to combine them all together in pursuit of a clearly stated aim'.

He analyses the innovations in four separate categories:

- the existence of a clearly stated aim from which much of the strategy followed
- the independent assertive role of the Directorate, which differed notably from the administrative secretariat models in other educational funding agencies
- the heavy emphasis on evaluation at four levels: by the Programme Committee, the Directorate, projects themselves and by two independent external agencies
- the inclusion of project management as a key criterion in selection and evolution of projects.

In the following sections we shall look closely at each of these areas and consider to what extent the innovations were welcome and successful.

### 3.4 Statement of aims

Educational planners and administrators have been wrestling unsuccessfully for a decade since the appearance of Planning Programming Budgeting Systems (PPBS) with the problems of defining and quantifying goals and objectives. Despite this, Richard Hooper decided in 1973 to make a clear statement of aims for the Programme and has in his *Final Report* asked to be judged against it. The principal aim he chose was 'To develop and secure the assimilation of computer assisted learning and computer managed learning on a regular institutional basis at reasonable cost' (Hooper, 1975).

By making institutionalization the key objective, various strategies for funding were inevitable given the tight timetable of the project. Projects were located in teaching departments and they were dissuaded from adopting unproven technology and untested educational approaches; there was a general trend (criticized by some outsiders) to 'play safe' in the selection of projects. The 'reasonable cost' wording led to other criteria: where possible the Programme chose to fund inter-institutional projects, which, while adding considerably to managerial and administrative complexities, have brought substantial gains in shared development costs; the emphasis on transfers of existing materials was another product which spawned a series of projects and a welcome concern with good documentation for all CAL and CML products. In the later years of NDPCAL some projects invested a heavy proportion of their time in the production and dissemination of packages. Several others never failed to criticize the package mentality which the Programme's stance initially encouraged. Hooper has now admitted that the transfer of ideas can be just as valuable as the transfer of packages and has thus corrected the earlier emphasis which may have led to wasted effort.

A further consequence of the principal aim was the emphasis on 'matched funding'; this is the investment in the project by the host institution of a roughly comparable sum to that provided by NDPCAL. The Directorate proved to be remarkably successful in getting institutions to show tangible support for their projects. Even though much of the matched funding represented hidden costs or 'funny money' rather than extra costs, the total of £2 million matched funding in the Programme (compared with £2.5 million from NDPCAL) proved a good indicator to institutional support. The identification of matched funding may have helped so many projects surmount the crucial takeover period after NDPCAL's demise, since some of them could continue with the same or less financial backing than before.

Project directors were fully conversant with the Programme's aims and philosophy because of the regular communications and newsletters, conferences, workshops and publications which the Directorate encouraged. There is clear evidence that they welcomed the emphasis on institutionalization and indeed one has complained that he did not get enough political support in his institution from NDPCAL. Another wrote that external funding 'has always been weak on the institutionalization side, after NDPCAL this weakness is of course apparent'.

The success or otherwise of the broad strategic aims of NDPCAL is considered elsewhere in this report (Chapter 8), in the Final Reports of the educational evaluation by Barry MacDonald and by the Director himself (Hooper, 1977). Even if judgement is possible on these matters, we cannot apportion responsibility for the outcome clearly between the Programme Committee and the Directorate.

### 3.5 Role of the Directorate

There is remarkable unanimity between Hooper and project directors about the role which the Directorate played in the management of NDPCAL. Hooper suggests that the Directorate was 'assertive' compared with the 'responsive' role of research council staff and one director thought the councils 'plump, passive and placid, whereas the NDP is lithe, vigorous and energetic'. Words like 'entrepreneurial', 'risk taking', and 'flexible' recur in the assessments which project staff made.

The active Directorate role was most noticeable in the formulation of project proposals for the consideration of the Programme Committee. Hooper saw this as a joint operation with the Directorate acting sometimes as editor, sometimes as producer and on occasions as marriage broker. Throughout there would be a developing dialogue between the Directorate and the project, as both sought to introduce their own priorities into the project design. Project directors thought this 'helpful and taken further in degree in NDPCAL than elsewhere', 'invaluable at the outset', 'very useful in having a good proposals mechanism and a policy so that the proposer doesn't waste too much time writing inappropriate tomes', and 'in strong contrast to other funding agencies which wait for applications'. One director thought the 'creation of projects through the identification of likely growth areas was impressive', but another thought that joint development could lead to misunderstanding and confusion.

Once a proposal was approved by the Programme Committee and the project was under way, the Directorate was more closely involved with the progress of the work than would be the case in most other agencies. Project staff seemed to welcome this: 'it could have been restrictive and oppressive; in fact it was helpful and supportive'. One way of maintaining contact was by attendance on project steering committees. This was variously considered 'helpful', 'well done as a project needs warning signals *and* time to get back on course', although NDPCAL is not necessarily unique in wanting membership on such committees. The closeness of the Directorate to projects led to the 'development of a sense of community through group meetings, newsletters and publicity generally'. Two factors assisted this: the homogeneity of projects already mentioned and the Directorate's open emphasis on regular travel between projects and encouragement of publicity and promotional skills. The open style of administration of the Programme was identified as a novel feature by project directors; one thought it 'refreshingly frank', while another noted that it may have enabled projects to put the Directorate right on some of their more serious misconceptions.

Criticism of the Directorate's style has focused on the general issue of managerial and financial controls. Several procedural innovations were identified by Hooper (which we consider in Section 3.7); these mostly owed their origins to the commercial world and were thus suspect to many academic staff in universities. Local authority projects, who were more familiar with line-item control over budgets by County Hall, took the procedures with greater equanimity. One project director thinks 'the NDP's organizational style in the first two years was characterized by lack of regard for the organizational problems in universities, and an aggressive attempt to dominate in detail the actual projects'. Dating from this period were efforts to impose technical standards for programming on all project staff, which met with almost universal rebellion. This showed conclusively how in educational funding the piper cannot always call the tune. The call for a standard approach to documentation and programming was certainly well intentioned, but it seemed to project staff to be the last straw in terms of central control and intervention for dubious benefit.

The image of an outsider imposing harsh managerial disciplines as the price for funding was not, we think, widely held. There is a classic rhetoric on this subject which springs quickly to the tongues of academic staff who wish to avoid accountability. We believe that the great majority of project staff acquiesced willingly in the managerial demands put on them after they had understood their rationale. As mentioned in Chapter 2, this was our experience in respect of the data we sought on academic staff time.

### 3.6 Evaluation

Richard Hooper has claimed that 'both the amount and types of evaluation used in the National Programme were unusual by comparison with traditional grant-giving agencies'. We doubt whether this claim can be questioned. Many projects appointed full-time evaluators and pursued rigorous programmes of formative evaluation of CAL material. The Directorate undertook a continual overall evaluation (in the managerial sense) but this was formalized at intervals in the mid-term evaluation and final review meetings. The Programme Committee were likewise continually evaluating the Programme, as they had the power at all times to initiate studies on its progress or failings. Finally, they decided to spend almost £200,000 on the two independent external evaluations undertaken, one by ourselves and the second by the Centre for Applied Research in Education at the University of East Anglia.

The two principal innovations in their spectrum are the appointment of external evaluators at the outset with different aspects of the evaluation to cover and the institution of the mid-term evaluation meetings. Clearly, we cannot comment on the success or otherwise of the two external evaluations and thus concentrate on the formal evaluation meetings. These were linked to a system of 'step funding', whereby projects were only given funds for a period of up to two years and a date was established, some six months or so before the end of the period, for a formal evaluation meeting. These lasted two days and often proved to be labour intensive and traumatic for project staff; conversely they were sometimes felt to be 'non-events'.

Project directors differ sharply in their assessment of these occasions. 'Most academics would find them an intolerable imposition'; 'it appeared time consuming, but it wonderfully concentrated our minds'; 'early warning of difficulties can be helpful; thus, provided it is done carefully and not overdone the "closer supervision" has been a useful feature of NDP'. There is no doubt that the existence of the mid-term evaluation sessions broke up the flow of some projects' productivity, diverted some staff time into administrative and data analysis activities and caused much extra work. They did, however, provide a useful opportunity to take stock, allowed external objective criticism to intrude and produced worthwhile data and presentational material for other audiences as well as for NDPCAL. The mid-term evaluations occasionally had teeth and at least two projects were not continued through to a second stage. Project directors were not expected by the Directorate to produce glossy documents for their mid-term evaluation, as no specific requirements were laid down. Knowing the Director's liking for polished presentations and audio-visual support, project directors produced a very high standard of written and visual material at the meetings. Much of the heavy time investment (which the staff time analysis showed) in the evaluation sessions may have been due to this pursuit of high standards.

### 3.7 Management procedures

The final area of innovation identified by Richard Hooper relates to management skills and procedures both in projects and in the Directorate. It is only here that there is any divergence between the views of Hooper and those of the project directors.

The innovations in question can be summarized as follows:

— the inclusion of managerial skills as a criterion for assessing project directors' worthiness to receive funds
— the pre-specification by projects of their educational and financial objectives
— the projection of financial requirements (for NDPCAL and the matched funding) for four-monthly periods throughout the term of the project
— the liberal use of 'virement' (the ability to transfer funds to an overspent category or heading from an underspent one)
— the requirement for regular reports with information on quantitative achievements (annual reports were requested where there was no evaluation meeting in the period).

The Directorate placed great store on good project management for reasons already implied: the short time scale, the large sum of resources involved, the inter-institutional complexity and the need for a visible record of alert management in case of failure. While project directors may have welcomed the powers and obligations given them, there is evidence that they found the frequent reporting restrictive. The following comments were received.

— 'Reporting procedures for NDP are much tighter than any I have encountered elsewhere, though somewhat relaxed from the early draconian attitude. In general, one accepts the irksome aspects as inevitable in a programme intended to work to a rigid timetable.'

— 'Record keeping and preparation of documents has absorbed too much staff time'.
— 'The stringent financial procedures have caused a lot of work without apparently compensatory benefits'.

NDPCAL had unusually heavy reporting obligations of its own. Unlike a Research Council it was investigating an area of endeavour in depth and had to produce summative statements about CAL and CML at the end of its life. To this extent the reporting requirements imposed on projects were specific and unlikely to be repeated. In addition, the financial and educational evaluations had data requirements which would not recur in conventional projects. As was mentioned in Chapter 2, the financial evaluation had to rely on project staff to collect and analyse its data. UNCAL made similar requests. The conjunction of all these demands produced an unusually heavy burden on projects. It is our view that, had projects been asked to meet only the requirements of NDPCAL (and not PMM and UNCAL) they would have found the administrative effort bearable.

The widespread use of virement in NDPCAL budgets has been universally welcomed. The Programme operated during a period of unprecedented price fluctuations and project directors found the facility to vire between headings to be extremely valuable.

**3.8 Transferability of the management innovations**

How novel are the management innovations that have been described? Do we accept Richard Hooper's suggestion that the only novelty lay in their coming together in one funding agency? If any of them are original, do they have relevance in other grant giving bodies?

If one allows for the special context in which NDPCAL operated (section 3.2), we believe that the innovations are different only in degree from similar practices in operation elsewhere. For example, the research councils allow some virement, but not as much as NDPCAL did; they ask for some budgetary projections, but without the detail and the time scale of NDPCAL. If British universities undertake research contracts for US Federal agencies, they have to complete statements which give the estimated contribution of the university. In view of the University Grants Committee's keen interest in the true cost of taking on external research, many universities prepare detailed internal assessments of their own 'matched funding' (Fielden and Lockwood, 1973). When we advised the Directorate on management and financial procedures in 1973, we based our recommendations on existing practices and tested them on some institutional administrators. As Hooper himself points out, the Nuffield Foundation has financed many inter-institutional projects, but they have not represented the greater proportion of their total funding, nor have they had strong pressures towards institutionalization built into them. Since the creation of the research initiative boards in the research councils their role has become more interventionist and creative.

Where NDPCAL has been clearly different is in its management style. One project director suggests that it 'has managed to create an aura of success and confidence'. In analysing the style we face the insuperable problem of disentangling the degree to which this is due to personalities or to decisions and procedures. One director finds the style 'so dependent on personality that I would hesitate to recommend it to anyone else. I fear that in general it would lead to restrictions and unhelpful control.' Another director echoes this feeling and suggests that, whereas all the special requirements of NDPCAL justified its practices, he would think them inapplicable *en masse* to research funding. There would be great difficulty finding personalities sensitive enough to modify NDPCAL's innovations to the more delicate world of research.

While we sympathize with this view, we do not agree fully with it. We believe that the key requirements for any transfer of NDPCAL's management innovations to any other area of research funding must be a limited homogeneous subject area and staff with sensitivity and entrepreneurial capabilities. Given these two features we consider that NDPCAL's experience has shown that the principles of accountability and management can be reconciled with the occasional volatility of research objectives and priorities. We see no reason why the concepts of matched funding, stepped funding, mid-term evaluations and project management should not be further applied (in a suitably modified form) to some areas of research. Clearly there will be instances where research activities appear as failures judged by purely managerial norms. In such cases the agency must have the knowledge and the sensitivity to identify those people who require backing as individuals, regardless of temporary setbacks to the successful progress of their research work. The application of these methods will often be little more than an increase in degree, where they already exist to some extent.

One of the major outcomes of the National Programme is its

experience and achievements in applying novel managerial approaches. Like UNCAL in their *Programme at Two* (UNCAL 1975) we believe that NDPCAL is 'a fascinating case study in the sociology of innovation'. We would go further and suggest that it has illustrated that a merger can be made between some managerial principles and the funding of academic research and development.

# PART B

# 4. Computer assisted learning (CAL)

## 4.1 CAL and the projects

Before looking at CAL projects we should first try to define CAL itself. Richard Hooper has produced a number of definitions and categorizations (Hooper, 1977). These emphasize the essential difference between CAL and CAI (computer assisted instruction) and programmed learning. British orthodoxy therefore sees CAL as being the use of the computer in the teaching-learning process in a variety of ways:

- to enhance understanding by simulating a process or experiment so that concepts and interactions are better appreciated
- to help mastery of technical or practical knowledge — sometimes referred to as 'drill and practice'
- to provide calculation and analysis facilities so as to remove the burdensome element from much tutorial and laboratory work and allow greater time for real learning
- to allow comparative experiences to be drawn upon by harnessing the data storage and analysis capabilities of the computer.

NDPCAL projects have sometimes used all of these approaches in their work; one, for example, has simulation packages, more routine examples for the students to practise with privately and an emphasis on tasks which require the writing of programs.

This financial evaluation is reporting on CAL and CML as exemplified by NDPCAL's projects. No data has been obtained from the many CAL activities outside the National Programme, since the evaluation was not in a position to ask for any special data collection and analysis.

Seventeen CAL projects were funded by NDPCAL. These are all explained briefly in Appendix C. They operated in the following areas:

- nine in higher and further education
- three in secondary schools
- two in industrial training
- three in military training (one Royal Navy, one Army, one Royal Air Force).

In this chapter we describe the 14 projects in the first three categories, while the three military projects are covered by Chapter 6 together with the military CML projects.

The fourteen projects cost at least £2,330,000 which, as shown in Table 1, comprised £1,238,000 from NDPCAL and at least £1,179,000 from the institutions themselves. As can be seen, they ranged substantially in expenditure from £463,000 to about £30,000 with the number of NDPCAL-funded staff varying from six to one. In educational terms the variations are also substantial; the CUSC Project's simulations on graphic display terminals have little in common with the Suffolk History Project's use of the ICL FIND package to help 12-year-olds answer questions on nineteenth-century village census returns.

The most homogeneous group of projects in NDPCAL's portfolio are the nine in universities and polytechnics; since their funding mostly began in 1973, they had almost all reached a steady state of development by 1977. It is possible therefore to make some generalizations about them and their continuing resource implications. The university-based projects were mostly inter-institutional in their initial design and some had used this concept vigorously to expand their student numbers. By mid-1977 the nine projects had 29 participating institutions and one, CALCHEM, had evolved a two-tier system with UK users of its computer system totalling 30.

The bulk of this chapter therefore relates to CAL in higher and further education. Some references are made to the two industrial training projects and the three schools projects, but we are reluctant to generalize on such small samples.

In the following sections we study some of the key questions about CAL:

— how does it affect conventional teaching? (Section 4.2)
— is it an extra or a replacement? (Section 4.3)
— how large a proportion of time will CAL take in a course? (Section 4.4)
— how long does it take to develop CAL? (Section 4.5)
— what are reasonable targets for terminal use? (Section 4.6)
— how much does CAL cost? (Section 4.7)
— how would CAL operate in a higher educational institution? (Section 4.8)
— what are the unit costs of CAL? (Section 4.9)
— how can the costs be minimized? (Section 4.10).

*Table 1. Funding (in thousands) for CAL (excluding three military projects)*

| *Project name* | *NDPCAL funding* | *Matched funding** | *Total* |
|---|---|---|---|
| | £ | £ | £ |
| *Higher and Further Education* | | | |
| Computer Based Learning Project (CBLP) | 157 | 138 | 295 |
| Engineering Sciences Project (ESP) | 221 | 178 | 399 |
| Computational Physics Teaching Laboratory (CPTL) | 49 | 87 | 136 |
| Clinical Decision Making | 64 | 35 | 99 |
| CALCHEM | 138 | 114 | 252 |
| MATLAB Project, Napier College | 134 | 133 | 267 |
| Computers in Undergraduate Science Curriculum (CUSC) | 216 | 247 | 463 |
| Basic Mathematics | 78 | 47 | 125 |
| CAL — a university service | 7 | 81 | 88 |
| *Secondary schools* | | | |
| Local History Classroom Project | 29 | † | 29 |
| CAL in Secondary School History | 12 | 9 | 21 |
| CAL in Upper School Geography | 40 | 6 | 46 |
| *Industrial Training* | | | |
| Management Decision Making | 79 | 76 | 155 |
| Post Office Technician Training | 14 | 28 | 42 |
| | 1,238 | 1,179 | 2,417 |

*Notes*

†Not available

*These figures have been provided by Project Directors according to guidelines set by the financial evaluation, but have not been checked for consistency

We conclude with two sections devoted to the special features of CAL in schools and industrial training.

## 4.2 The identification of changes due to CAL

One of the hardest questions for the evaluation to answer has been: what is the nature of the change? In some projects there is no simple answer since CAL material has been used differently according to the teacher's preferences and teaching style and according to the CAL package or simulation in question. Surrey University's CPTL project for example identified at least four different modes of use of the computer. Since the nature of the change will directly influence the impact on resources, it is important to identify the types of use. The following types have been found.

- Timetabled attendance at terminals instead of previously timetabled lectures, tutorial sessions, examples classes or laboratory experiments.
- Timetabled attendance at terminals as an extra to an unchanged curriculum; here the CAL sessions are used to supplement and reinforce conventional teaching.
- Untimetabled free access to terminals for specific project work based on CAL programs or calculation and simulation facilities. In this case the terminal has probably replaced some other resources previously required for the project.
- Free access to terminals by students for revision purposes towards the end of the academic year.
- Terminals available as a teaching aid in the lecture theatre, examples class or experimental laboratory. In some instances the students could be required to use the terminal to solve a practical problem in the class; CAL will be an extra input to the teaching process and may, as with some CALCHEM packages, help students prepare for laboratory experiments.
- Use of the computer in batch mode to answer specific questions relating to work in a class or tutorial session. In the Suffolk History project such use was optional, while in Imperial College's Fluid Mechanics programs for the ESP project the computer had become the focal part of the whole course.

When individual teachers use packages in different ways in their own individual courses, the change will be discernible only to that one academic. Thus, a financial evaluation which attempted to draw up precise balance sheets before and after the change would rapidly become too deeply involved in detail with serious data problems.

### 4.3 Is CAL an extra or a substitution?

This question is at the heart of the resource evaluation and is extremely complex. It is essential to distinguish between addtional time of staff or students and additional costs. Some projects have no marginal effect on time, but are a considerable cost burden. Others are an extra in both senses. As a result of the final reviews we identified the following position in CAL projects:

— Clinical Decision Making project — the use of the terminal replaces time spent by students either at the bedside in wards or in GPs' consulting rooms

— Glasgow Mathematics — mathematics units replace problem hours, but are extra formal 'contact' time as far as the students are concerned

— Upper School Geography — each educational unit is appropriate for one to three hours' sixth-form classroom work and can be used by students without access to a computer or an understanding of computing; thus the units replace other teaching material at an extra cost

— CUSC — the project suggests that virtually all the CAL use is a replacement of normal student activity, except at Surrey where some 400 student-hours per annum are additional

— CPTL, Surrey — most of the students' attendance in the CPTL is a replacement for conventional lectures or represents free use of the system; however, 25 hours extra per student are timetabled over the first two years of the course for the voluntary use of specific CAL packages

— Suffolk and Clwyd history projects — teachers use the computerized data base when they wish to answer specific questions during classes on local history

— CALCHEM project — in most cases the packages supplement and support existing laboratory experiments, but few instances exist of packages reducing demand for staff contact time and replacing tutorial or examples classes

— CBLP project, Leeds — the terminal contact is mostly extra for students, although in two (of the 12) user departments it has replaced examples classes

— Napier College MATLAB project — the packages are normally used during mathematics examples classes under supervision of the class teacher
— Management Decision Making — the system is an extra resource in existing case study periods on a course or forms the focus of a short special-purpose course by itself.

Finally, one project, the Engineering Sciences Project, exemplifies our dilemma. In some institutions, notably Queen Mary College and the University of Exeter, some of the packages have replaced laboratory sessions, while in four other institutions other packages proved an extra facility which enhances students' understanding.

This latter point brings us to the question of educational impact as opposed to resource impact. The financial evaluation has tried to separate the two perspectives in considering the question of extra and replacement. We have naïvely assumed that CAL will always be different from anything it replaces, but are not competent to measure the change. Thus, where a replacement occurs we have tried to measure the changed 'inputs', but not the changed outcomes. Where CAL is an extra, we have identified the extra resources, but not the extra or changed educational values.

We can conclude that CAL is used both to add to and to replace existing teaching methods. There has been evidence to suggest that teachers are initially reluctant to adopt CAL as a formal part of any course while it is untried and relatively unknown. There is therefore a predictable cycle of adoption in which CAL material is introduced to the fringes of a course by enthusiasts as an extra, slowly gains adherents and respect and then becomes adopted formally in a course, replacing some other teaching method. As the National Programme was pioneering and developmental, it is not unreasonable to expect it to have a higher proportion of 'extra' or fringe projects than a similar agency would have in ten years' time.

### 4.4 Hours of CAL and its impact on staff and students

The American experience led some observers to expect that CAL in Britain would be replacing conventional teaching activity on a large scale and that the numbers of hours of tutorials saved would inevitably lead to calls from governments and administrators for staff reductions. As a result of NDPCAL's activities we can conclusively refute such suggestions on the grounds of scale and development costs. It seems unlikely that student contact with terminals will exceed 40 hours per annum and a typical use in the foreseeable future is likely to be between ten and twenty hours per student. From the higher education projects, we have culled the following statistics on student contact:

- — a maximum of 34 hours per annum for engineering students including some time devoted to instruction on programming (Exeter/ESP)
- — ten of the formal seventy hours which medical students spend in the General Practice Department (Clinical Decision Making)
- — students would take an average of eight units per annum (about ten to eight hours in total) (Glasgow Mathematics)
- — the use of the 46 packages is unlikely to be more than 2% of the formal class time in a student's year (CALCHEM)
- — the project envisages a possible plateau of 12 hours per annum of CAL service teaching for up to 1000 students (CBLP)
- — use of the terminal will not normally occupy more than 50% of the examples class time allocated to a particular topic (Napier — MATLAB); in general, MATLAB packages will be applicable to between 10% and 30% of the content of existing mathematics courses
- — students are timetabled for 78 hours of CAL during their first two years, but 28 hours of this is for voluntary use of packages (CPTL).

Some of these student hours have been dearly bought and the total investment in development is considerable. Because of this we doubt whether CAL material will regularly form more than 10% of formal teaching contact.

The impact of the change on staff and student time clearly depends on the extent to which CAL material is replacing former instruction or is an additional option. Even where it is wholly additional, we can see on the basis of the existing CAL projects that it seems unlikely to exceed one hour per week of extra contact for an individual student (assuming a 26-week teaching year). Only if CAL were to become less labour intensive in its programming and development and terminals were to fall in price do we believe that it would be used to a greater extent with students. The extra load on academic staff will be linked to other factors such as class size, number of terminals, their availability, timetable constraints, and, if CAL is replacing something, the staff-student load of that activity being replaced. In addition, teaching methods with CAL are still at the development stage. Many projects are finding that students can work very effectively in pairs at a terminal, although the effectiveness will depend to a large extent on the package's content and style. Some project directors found it essential to phase out academic staff supervision of students because staff could not afford the time for supervising small groups at terminals. This was particularly necessary in laboratory projects with a limited number of graphic display terminals. In these cases a staff member was being asked to substitute for one afternoon in a conventional laboratory a whole series of sessions at terminals which would take up a much greater share of his time.

We believe we can generalize and say that in most of NDPCAL's higher education projects terminals are unsupervised by academic staff. Thus, where the CAL session is substituting for another activity, staff time has been released. We have shown what a small proportion of contact time this is. We believe it is usually reallocated to tutorial effort related to the CAL packages or to the development of further material. Our evidence from the projects hardly supports the notion of a rush to adopt CAL because of the free time and leisure it brings:

- at Leeds three teachers said that use of the statistics materials had increased their workload since they spent time preparing individual 'control programs' fitting in their own approach to the modules and material available
- in the CUSC project there is a small increase of a few per cent in academic workload, which at Surrey has involved an extra hour of demonstrating in laboratories
- in the Physics Department at Surrey the contact hours of the six members of staff involved in the mathematics course have increased by about 350 hours a year because of the small class sizes in the terminal room — this increased load has fallen particularly heavily on two or three of the staff, yet the 25 staff in the department were not expected by the head of the department (also the project director) to have to give more than 10% extra contact time on average
- medical students in Glasgow are supervised by staff at the terminal during the first year that they encounter CAL. In their final two years they work unsupervised.

### 4.5 Development times for CAL material

One aspect of CAL which the evaluation was determined to study carefully was its development cost. Was it going to be like some other educational technologies which required one hundred hours of time to create one serviceable hour of product? Table 2 below gives the answers from some of the higher educational projects.

*Table 2. Package development times.*

| *Project* | *Total time in hours* | *Academic time included in total* |
|---|---|---|
| Engineering Sciences Project | approx 400 | approx 10% |
| CUSC | 50-500 | 10% |
| CALCHEM | 200-300 | 16% |
| Glasgow Mathematics | approx 240 | 50% |
| CPTL | approx 100 | approx 70% |

Data are not shown for all projects, since the concept of a package is not applicable to them all and there is also the obvious problem of the differing scale and sophistication of packages produced. Some of the packages can provide up to two or three hours of tuition for a student (ESP Engineering Sciences Project at Queen Mary College) others may last only twenty minutes or so. Thus, the discrepancy in the development times is often related directly to package duration. Clearly it takes longer to prepare (and document) programs with more than, say, 3000 lines of coding than the small ones of 100 lines. Two projects have amply demonstrated the huge range of development times in relatively homogeneous projects. In CALCHEM, for example, four packages have absorbed more than 600 hours of time, nine required under 100 hours, but the bulk were in the range from 200-400 hours. CUSC has a similar spread.

As a further aid to understanding development time, John Peterson (1977) has analysed the size of 451 programs written with NDPCAL funds. He found that the range of sizes, measured in lines of coding, was vast (from 50 lines to 10,000), that the mean size was 714, the median about 400 and the mode 100 lines. He also suggested that it would be wrong to assume that CAL programs in NDPCAL were typically written in FORTRAN and BASIC. As many programs were written in special-purpose CAL languages as in the two well-known ones.

The National Programme was generous to some projects in the provision of technical assistance in the form of programmers. It was clear that they did the bulk of the programming and in one sense Hooper's liberality made eventual takeover of active development a less likely proposition. His *Final Report* estimated that 20-30 out of the 100 staff funded by NDPCAL would be funded by their institutions after January 1978. Thus, some development will continue, but at a greatly reduced rate. The low proportionate involvement by academic staff in package development, shown in Table 2, poses problems for the future. It would be not unreasonable to conclude that the development of CAL programs is not possible on any scale without specialist programmer support. Where this cannot be provided by internal reallocation of tasks among central programming staff or by external funding, it is unlikely that academic staff can fill the gap. In a time of no growth or cutback, the implications of this are severe unless CAL is seen to rank high in institutional priorities.

One feature of American experience which was thought likely to recur in Britain was the existence of a learning curve in package development. As programmers and academic staff gain experience of CAL, is one not justified in expecting quicker production? Project staff do not endorse this theory, but suggest that the production-line analogy is wholly irrelevant, since the individual programmer is not in that kind of environment. Packages will become increasingly complex and programmers will seek fresh challenges once they have mastered the easier work. It would be unrealistic in view of this to expect any great reduction in development times in the near future.

The length of the package development times has undoubtedly been increased by NDPCAL's emphasis on the thorough documentation of programs. While initial attempts at codifying and standardizing the work of all the programmers failed to be accepted by project staff, they have none the less given very considerable time to formalizing documentation procedures. The results are impressive and there is no doubt that the extra effort which this required has saved time in some inter-institutional projects. We consider this more fully in Chapter 7.

**4.6 Terminals and timetables**

CAL projects have used a variety of terminals ranging from simple ASR and KSR teletypes to graphics visual display units. Their costs have risen steadily throughout the period because of inflation and sterling devaluation. Thus, NDPCAL paid £920 for the simplest teletype in January 1977 compared with £580 three-and-a-half years earlier. Richard

Hooper emphasized the cost factor in negotiations with projects over terminal numbers and the evaluation also has concentrated on getting reliable data on the use of terminals. This information will help future CAL users plan their terminal requirements. Table 3 below shows the annual usage per terminal of the principal large CAL projects.

*Table 3. Average annual use per terminal in hours (1976-77).*

| *Project* | *Comments* |
|---|---|
| Engineering Sciences Project | 320 hours in one institution (others lower) |
| CPTL | 550 hours' use by students |
| CUSC (Surrey only) | 190 hours (other institutions are lower) |
| CBLP (Leeds) | 260 hours |
| CALCHEM (Leeds only) | 300 hours (other institutions report lower use) |
| Clinical Decision Making | 150 hours (one hospital only) |

In making forecasts of the likely level of terminal use both the financial evaluation and project directors have proved consistently wrong. In 1969 an NCET feasibility study postulated an average use of 2000 terminal hours per annum (NCET, 1969). In 1974 we suggested that 750 hours was a realistic target for project directors. We now consider 500 hours more achievable, as this represents 19 hours per week during a 26-week teaching year. The Leeds statistics project with many classes of 50 to 60 social sciences students has proved a reliable indicator. The director initially thought a 25-hour-per-week target was readily achievable, since the students were not bound by inflexible laboratory timetables and in Leeds University there were two terminal rooms in different locations. In practice, however, the highest weekly utilization of any one of the four terminal rooms has been 14.6 hours at Bradford University in the spring term of 1976 and this was said to be causing the teaching staff some concern. The 550 hours per terminal achieved by the Surrey CPTL project are due to the substantial untimetabled element in the usage, which in 1976-77 represented 49% of the total hours. (Table A.3 in Appendix A).

Projects which have incorporated CAL materials into the laboratory time on a course have found that the inevitable timetabling difficulties restrict their potential use of terminals. Although, in theory, students in laboratory-based disciplines would be able to use terminals during the mornings, they usually regard lectures as essential commitments. CAL packages which relate directly to or substitute for laboratory experiments require the student's presence in the laboratory, which, in turn, may involve the presence of technicians. The packages are thus sometimes restricted in availability to the afternoons only at a time in the course when they are relevant to the subject content. In the CALCHEM project, for example, the packages relating to physical chemistry were only of use to students for seven to eight weeks of their year.

Further factors affecting terminal use are:

- building security and janitorial working hours: untimetabled free access by students after five o'clock in the evening may be impossible because of administrative hurdles (one institution cited an insurance company's restriction on hours of computer use as a possible constraint)
- the need for technical assistance (or academic supervision)
- the geographical location of terminals and the length of packages (a one-hour gap between lectures cannot accommodate a 50-minute package in a terminal room ten minutes' walk away)
- the atmosphere and facilities of the terminal room (one project has stressed the need for automatic coffee dispensers to calm students waiting for access to terminals)
- the reliability of the hardware against shut-downs or faults
- the encouragement of attendance by individual academic staff who may or may not incorporate references to CAL packages and their value in their lectures.

Before condemning directors of CAL projects for squandering precious resources by under-utilizing terminals, one should look closely at the use given to other equally precious resources in higher education. The University Grants Committee has stated as an objective that laboratory places should be used for an average of 16 hours per week. In practice, the real utilization is lower in many engineering and science departments (Dunworth, 1974). One effect that could therefore become evident in future is that terminal rooms will have a higher average use than other academic accommodation. This means that, where the CAL material is replacing conventional teaching, the average use of other accommodation will fall slightly. Where CAL provides extra student contact, this will not be the case.

**4.7 The cost of CAL at three levels**

In Chapter 3 we outlined the methodology we have developed for assessing the cost impact of CAL and CML. This involves producing answers for three levels of inquiries, at the school or departmental level, at the institution or local education authority level, and at the national level. Not all the answers are in financial units and all vary greatly in size. In very broad terms the answers for CAL can be summarized as follows.

— Academic departments or schools can carry out CAL activities at little or no marginal financial cost. The cash demands on them are unlikely to exceed the cost of maintenance of a dedicated computer and terminals. The major demand will be in programmer and teaching staff time to develop (and sometimes maintain) the CAL systems.

— Institutions and authorities may also find that the marginal cost of CAL is low if they have a under-utilized computer and terminals. Not until the activity expands to demand additional staff, space or hardware does the impact become clearer. We show later that at this stage a central CAL service for the institution could cost approximately £20,000 a year extra.

— In cost-per-student-hour terms CAL is more expensive than conventional instruction except in the case of some laboratory applications. Total costs range from £4 to more than £15 per student-terminal-hour (one student at one terminal for one hour).

What the three-level approach has done is to emphasize the different conclusions at the three levels. In a department the innovation is cheap, exciting and may produce some tangible benefits (as well as educational gains). For the institution the full cost implications will take some time to appear and a large part of the cost (the time invested in development activity) will always be hidden. Only at the national level can we see a full cost picture but this is in terms which mean little to local decision-makers.

The effect of these three levels is that decisions will often be taken in the existing budgetary decision-making structure without an appreciation of the total costs. Some budgetary structures may even actively distort the true picture. One example is an NDPCAL school-based project which decided to charge teachers 75p per pupil per annum for providing printed worksheets and handouts. The teachers complained at the sum which must be found from their departmental funds. The worksheets, which are in effect largely replacing the teachers' own effort, require spirit duplicator materials and printing paper. These are drawn from the school's stationery stores at no charge to teachers and no records are maintained of the total use by departments. The NDPCAL project is probably thus causing an overall fall in demand for school resources, but its actual resource impact on the school will be calls from departments for more funds to help meet the cost of the worksheets. If extra money is not forthcoming, the project will in some cases not be continued as departments cannot find the 75p per student from their own resources.

### 4.8 CAL in an institution of higher education

Staff in three CAL projects reported at the final review meetings that future participation in CAL activities after January 1978 would cost their departmental budgets nothing. They represented fifteen institutions. Even where some expenses are being passed on, as in the inter-institutional charges that Leeds University is making to Leeds Polytechnic and Bradford University, the level of marginal costs does not exceed £1.70 per student-terminal-hour for 1977/78. In Exeter University the marginal cost of 4500 student-terminal-hours to the Engineering Sciences Department in 1978 is expected to be about £4000 even though the department has a dedicated minicomputer. At the University of Surrey the extra cost of the CPTL to the Physics Department will amount to £7900 in 1978, which represents about £1.40 per student-hour.

In an institution the cost of CAL clearly depends on the organization it establishes for providing computer time. If departments or faculties are enthusiastic enough to acquire their own minicomputers (from central equipment grant allocations) the university or polytechnic will find little drain on its funds. Not until the CAL demands of departments justify the provision of a central CAL service will the resource implications become more tangible. This has already happened in four of NDPCAL's projects. The most common pattern is for a central CAL service to develop under the aegis of the institution's computer centre. A medium to large minicomputer is acquired and specific staff allocated to provide CAL services on it. As an illustration of the costs that might be involved, we show in Table 4 below the two possible models for the provision of CAL.

*Table 4. Typical CAL costs in a higher educational institution (1977).*

| | *Central service* | *Departmental or faculty minicomputer* |
|---|---|---|
| | £ | £ |
| *Capital costs* | | |
| Computer and peripherals | 60,000 | 20,000 |
| Graphic display terminals | 17,500 | 7,000 |
| Teletypes or VDUs | 20,000 | 10,000 |
| | 97,500 | 37,000 |
| *Extra operating costs* | | |
| Computer maintenance | 6,000 | 2,000 |
| Terminal maintenance | 2,600 | 1,200 |
| Programmers, operators | 12,000 | 6,000 |
| Other costs (insurance, etc) | 1,000 | 500 |
| | 21,600 | 9,700 |

The figures in Table 4 relate only to tangible extra costs and do not include the variable costs of operation and hidden costs such as academic staff time, the time of staff in the central computer centre, space and other overheads. The two models we have shown would provide 12,500 and 6000 terminal-hours of time approximately, assuming the average terminal utilization was 500 hours per annum in each case.

### 4.9 What are the unit costs of CAL?

The method we have used to calculate total national costs per student hour has been described in Chapter 2. We are reluctant to compare the national total cost of one project with another, since each project's outcomes are so different in nature, scale and sophistication, even if they could be measured. It is instructive, nonetheless, to look at the absolute figures and ranges of annual total cost and to see the share taken by the three principal elements. Thus, in Table 5 we show the total costs of seven CAL projects calculated for 1977/78 after NDPCAL funding has stopped. In some cases the figures relate to one participating institution rather than to the project as a whole, since average or composite figures would be misleading.

*Table 5. Analysis of total national costs of some CAL projects (estimates 1977/78).*

| Project code | Depreciation on capital | Operating costs | Year's share (20%) of past development expenditure | Total cost |
|---|---|---|---|---|
| | £ | £ | £ | £ |
| A | 2,450 | 2,950 | 6,330 | 11,730 |
| B | 6,600 | 24,050 | 12,150 | 42,800 |
| C | 8,020 | 14,800 | 11,700 | 34,520 |
| D | 2,650 | 4,800 | 3,250 | 10,700 |
| E | 12,000 | 13,000 | 3,300 | 28,300 |
| F | 4,600 | 17,700 | 10,500 | 32,800 |
| G | 3,100 | 12,400 | 13,000 | 28,500 |

Although these figures are barely meaningful in isolation, they do show that the development costs comprise a substantial proportion (usually between 30% and 50%) of the total. Since the annual development charge is one-fifth of the accumulated development expenditure, we can put this another way and say that the total development will represent between twice and five times the annual operating cost and depreciation charges added together. It is possible to reduce development costs substantially, as Project E has done, by relying on imported algorithms as the basis for developing packages.

Although we are reluctant to quote project costs per student-terminal-hour, we can cite the range and the most common costs derived in our calculations. We find that the lowest total cost predicted for 1977/78 was just under £4 per student-terminal-hour, while most CAL projects' costs were in the range of £5 to £15 per hour. Several projects showed cost figures far in excess of £15, but there were special circumstances for most of these. In some of these latter cases we were not convinced that the project had reached its steady state as regards student numbers. The unit costs we have quoted do not take account of three factors, since we can see no way of including them.

— The student-hours of use (and related costs) by institutions outside the projects who have taken over their material. If we are to achieve a genuine national cost we should identify all users of the packages produced. Non-project users have been reluctant to provide information on the extent of their use, even though NDPCAL projects have tried to insist on this feedback as the price for free CAL material.
— The use of CAL in lectures as a teaching aid. If 100 students see a package used to supplement a lecturer's presentation, we consider it unrealistic to count this as 100 student-terminal-hours.
— The financial saving from any activity that has been replaced by CAL. This omission could be significant where the project's materials are replacing conventional methods. In Section 4.2 we outlined some of the difficulties in identifying the change, which could ultimately involve a detailed study of individual academic staff workloads; in view of these problems and the subsequent methodological difficulties of attaching costs to these activities, we have not reduced the CAL cost figure given in Table 5 for time replaced.

The unit costs we have derived should be set in the context of the costs of their surrounding activities. Thus, if it costs £30,000 to produce one medical graduate, a higher CAL unit cost might be justified than in, say, a social science project. We consider this later in Chapter 8 in the context of conventional teaching costs, where we ask whether NDPCAL is producing value for money.

**4.10 Ways of minimizing the cost of CAL**

Our review of the fourteen CAL projects has enabled us to pinpoint ways of minimizing costs. We place these factors in five groups related to the number of students, the use of computers, terminals, the choice of topic and academic staff.

— Student numbers are the crucial element in unit cost calculations. Projects which have tried to market their products to increase their student audience have reduced unit costs. One simple way of achieving large numbers is to convert packages requiring staff supervision into unsupervised exercises. When staff are no longer required to attend in terminal rooms, they may be happier to ask for more CAL sessions on the timetable. If students sit at a terminal in twos or threes, there is also an immediate boost to numbers. This also enables CAL packages to be timetabled closer to the related lecture or seminar sessions.

— The use of hardware radically affects the incidence of costs; even though the two models in Table 4 produce similar overall unit costs, it can clearly be financially advantageous for a department to use a central CAL service as fewer of the costs will reach its own budget. The department should then consider its mode of operation: could CAL be operated in batch mode? Are on-line terminals really necessary? If programs are to be developed the choice of language is vital, as it will influence development times, the attitude of interested academic staff and the ability to import material developed elsewhere.

— Factors relating to the use of terminals have been discussed in section 4.5. They included geographical location and layout of the terminal room, its availability outside peak hours and the reliability and ease of comprehension of the equipment by students.

— The choice of topic for a CAL unit or package can radically influence the number of staff wishing to use it in their courses. Packages which cover subjects which are controversially treated, parochial, too ephemeral or too long in duration will not prove popular. Some projects have spent hundreds of hours developing material only to find that it had few sponsors; others obtained sponsors at the outset and ensured that the topics chosen were found in many syllabi and were generally areas where the special features of CAL would make a contribution to learning or to clarifying understanding.

— The amount of staff involvement in development and the degree to which other departmental staff know about CAL are crucial elements. Much duplication of development effort can be saved by the import of ideas, if not packages, into a department. On the other hand material will gain readier acceptance if all the potential users are consulted about it at the developmental stage so that they feel involved in its creation. The internal political influence in academic decision-making of those involved is also important; a very quick way to ensure that CAL material is used is to make it a formal rather than optional part of the course. This was the position in 1977 in most of the CAL projects.

While CAL is still at the developmental stage, many of its initial successes will owe much to the enthusiasm and dedication of individual entrepreneurs. This excess energy and zeal cannot always be repeated in future projects and our assessments of NDPCAL's projects must be discounted to allow for this factor. Their experiences have been heavily chronicled in this and other reports and if future CAL enthusiasts wish to benefit from the years 1973-77 they could find much recorded that will help them.

### 4.11 CAL in schools

The three schools projects are dissimilar from those in higher education. The two history projects treat the computer as an extra resource primarily for its data storage and analytical capabilities. Terminals have only been used experimentally (and then by teachers rather than students) as most of the development has been based on batch use. When terminals were used (in Clwyd) many practical problems arose related to noise, availability of the terminal, its siting in a classroom and the management of the class.

In our assessment of these two projects we used cost per inquiry as the most suitable measure, since the final mode of operation in both cases involved teachers collecting questions from pupils and putting them into a format suitable for computer input. The postal service was then used to convey the questions to and from the computer. We found that such a service could be operated in one county for a marginal cost (from the county treasurer's viewpoint) of about £3 to £4 per question. The benefits claimed are that the computer has saved children from detailed analysis and transcription of census records and that the analytical capability allows the teacher to get his pupils to 'write history'.

The Upper School Geography project uses the computer as a resource producer. Units from the project do not require any class contact with the computer, but are produced on the demand of the teacher, suitably adapted for his particular syllabus and geographical locality. Each unit will be used as a basis for sixth-form work for up to three hours. The saving arises because teachers no longer have to develop materials for these classroom periods and can have units specially generated for their individual purposes.

### 4.12 CAL in industrial training

The two NDPCAL projects in this area offer no base for generalizations.

The Management Decision Making project (MDM) at the London Business School has not followed its planned course of development and maintains that it has not finally solved the complex educational issues involved. The other at the Post Office did not continue for a year after an initial feasibility study, but is now reconsidering a further stage of development and application. Training applications of CAL are seen as the major area for expansion by both Hazeltine and Control Data Corporation for their TICCIT and PLATO systems respectively. It is thus particularly unfortunate that NDPCAL's experience does not help us to assess the potential for CAL in this area.

The MDM project developed computer programs which could be used in a range of management training courses to teach understanding of decision-making processes. The project's materials aim to enable individuals to understand other people's concepts and perceptions of their own position. The computer creates a context in which individuals can learn; it does not replace the teacher, but gives him a tool which he uses to help students. The programs are of two types basically — simulations of industries with role playing and games in syndicates and content-free programs, which allow pairs of students to test their grasp of conceptual understanding.

The MDM project has used its materials on 25 different courses with an average of 20 students each. On each course the material has differed, as it has been continually developing. The teacher uses a terminal on-line to the LBS computer and puts students' material in batches himself. In some courses the introductory lectures, the simulations and games take up as much as two-and-a-half days. During this time only one staff member has been needed and the project can thus claim a gain as the staff investment needed for an average LBS class of 20 would be at least two. The project has spent much effort in seeking to promote its ideas and find places on courses for its products. As a result of this, ten institutions are currently interested in MDM programs. Since the project always had a low proportion of its total student contact hours in its home base (LBS), the director was forced to play a demanding peripatetic role.

The other industrial project was based at the Post Office's South Western Regional Training Centre and was concerned with the training of technicians in the maintenance of customers' equipment. Time was bought on the South Western Electricity Board's computer, which was used via a telephone link, and IBM's Interactive Training System (ITS) was employed. A particular course, which had already been analysed and rewritten into a largely programmed learning format, was chosen. The course elements were modified for computer use by the Training Centre staff. The CAL modules incorporated pre-and post-tests and multi-choice questions and included simulations of equipment faults. The computer was also used for course management, routing trainees between modules and maintaining performance records. The system was run with over 60 students and a detailed comparison was made with a control group which received conventional instruction. The results of the two groups matched very closely in terms of attainment, but there was evidence of a significant improvement in the speed of learning in the theoretical aspects of the course under the computer system. On this course the theoretical content accounted for only a small part of the time; there seems more potential for an improvement in the quality of training and in the better use of instructional resources on some of the more advanced courses. The Post Office are now planning to take the approach further by running trials on a higher level course. This will use their own computer which will enable them to exploit the ITS facilities more fully.

### 4.13 Conclusion

CAL is now a tried supplement and alternative to conventional teaching. 35,000 student-terminal-hours were recorded in 1976/77 in the projects we have reviewed. While we have shown that it is nearly always more expensive in total cost terms than existing methods, there are many cases where the particular marginal costs of adopting CAL in the institution are low. In terms of extra cost CAL could cost less than extra teaching staff. The educational evaluation is reporting on the qualitative aspects of the change. There are many claims for added educational value, enhanced understanding, immediacy, flexibility, etc, which require examination. When answers are received to these questions, the decision-maker can then face the ultimate value judgement. Is the probable extra cost of CAL worth the extra claimed educational value?

# 5. Computer managed learning (CML) in higher and secondary education

## 5.1 Introduction

This chapter deals with the use of the computer as an aid to educational management. It does not cover standard commercial applications or the use of the computer, for example, by university libraries; although this type of use is widespread in educational institutions and authorities, it has little to do with the learning process and the National Programme has not invested any of its funds in the area.

Computer managed learning (CML) however is relevant to the Programme's activities and it is with this type of application that this chapter is mainly concerned. CML usually refers to the management of learning at the micro level (that is dealing with the detailed components of individual students' work at frequent intervals) and performs some of the functions of recording, marking, assessing, directing or recommending and reporting. Two other projects which are rather more administrative in their nature are covered at the end of the chapter: one is the use of a CML system at a macro level to manage students' records and the other is the use of the computer in school timetabling. Military projects are not included here but covered separately in Chapter 6.

CML applications are usually fairly major ventures and can take a long time to develop and implement. The structure of a whole course, or a significant part of it, is often completely reworked and there is less opportunity for gradual or piecemeal introduction of packages as can often be done with CAL; also very complex computer software systems are involved. For these reasons hardly any of NDPCAL's CML projects are yet in a steady state; this and the fact that there are only one or two projects in any one educational area makes it impossible to generalize with CML.

## 5.2 Need for CML

In higher education there has in recent years been an increasing emphasis on individual learning and modular courses, often crossing traditional subject boundaries. The individual student is more responsible for deciding the nature of his own course by choosing combinations of optional units; these often make considerable use of self-study and can attempt to accommodate different learning styles by the use of multi-media resources in place of traditional lectures and print-based material.

This type of learning can bring severe management problems for the teacher who may be dealing with large numbers of students moving at different speeds and by different routes through several courses. Depending on the circumstances, there can be a need for some or all of the following facilities which might be provided by a CML system.

*Student records.* Maintaining records of a student's progress through the course and his attainment within individual units and on the course as a whole.

*Routing.* To direct or recommend the next unit, or choice of units for study or for remedial work. The routing may depend not only on the student's expressed preference but also on pre- and post-requisites for the individual modules and on the course structure (typically, some modules will constitute a compulsory core and some units may depend on the student having already completed other work, so that there can be several constraints on routing choice).

*Testing.* With individual course structure and progress there is a consequent need for frequent individual testing, usually at the end of each unit. The computer can play a part in this by presenting a selection of multi-choice questions from item banks and automatically marking them; the student's responses may be made directly on mark-sensed cards which can be read by the computer's input device.

*Question analysis.* The responses to computer-based questions can be analysed statistically in order to improve the effectiveness of this type of testing. Questions may be analysed, for example, in terms of their general difficulty using a 'facility index' or in terms of their power to differentiate sharply over a range of student ability by using a 'discrimination index'.

*Teacher and student reports.* The student may need reports in detail on his work and in general on his progress in the course. The teacher needs general reports on whole courses and the ability to call for detailed reports on individual students, units or examinations.

In secondary, as distinct from higher, education the need for CML arises from the requirement within the school system for mixed-ability teaching. Given the decision to adopt mixed-ability teaching there can be severe problems for the teacher in the organization of the children's work. One approach is in the use of more individualized learning where the pupils work at different paces and to different levels, making use of more self-teaching material. This in turn can bring problems of classroom management as there is a need for the teacher to be free to spend more time on helping children individually than is the case with more homogenous groups where most problems can be dealt with on a class basis.

This type of teaching needs very careful organization if the bright child is not to run out of allotted work or the less able to lose his momentum in the backwater of one particular problem area for lack of individual attention. The teacher ideally needs up-to-date records of the progress of each pupil, and also help in the routine tasks of setting and marking the frequent tests in order to identify the pupils' strengths and weaknesses and hence to decide on their next unit of work. It is in these areas that some educational workers have looked to the computer for help in the secondary classroom.

Thus although the reasons leading to the introduction of CML are different in emphasis in higher and secondary education, the requirements of a practical system are similar in both areas. There are of course differences of detail with, for example, less complex routing in the secondary level. In both cases however, the introduction of a CML system usually requires the development of educational material in addition to the computer system. The curriculum needs to be broken down into units suitable for computer management, pre- and post-test requirements must be specified and the material written or presented in a way suitable for self-study. This is an important point in evaluating CML systems: usually a vast amount of curriculum development goes hand in hand with the system development. There are exceptions to this, where a course already exists in a self-study, modular fashion but is being managed manually; or where all the facilities of a CML system are not appropriate — for example, in a course which is in discrete units but conventionally taught, the main requirements might be simply for test marking and analysis.

## 5.3 Methods of CML

There are two basic approaches to developing CML systems. One is the individually tailored or 'content-specific' system which is produced for one particular application; the other is the general or 'content-free' system which has no inbuilt requirements of course content, type of reporting or other factors but which aims to be easily adaptable by any user to his own particular needs. As in other computer applications, each method has its advantages and drawbacks. The tailor-made system is in principle capable of being more efficient at the job for which it was designed; it should meet the user's needs more fully and with less redundancy of facilities and capacity. The content-free system on the other hand should, in the long run, lead to lower development costs and might on some occasions provide facilities which it would be too expensive to develop specifically for an individual application. Unlike CAL, most CML applications do not use interactive computing or computer terminals but rely on batch processing, often with an overnight turn-round and postal or courier delivery if the computer is not on the same site as the teaching.

### 5.4 The CAMOL system

Probably the most important CML development in this country, and the largest project in the National Programme's portfolio, is CAMOL (Computer Management of Learning) which is a large content-free ICL system. Most of the systems development, programming and testing has been carried out by ICL but some parts of it, together with the educational material required to instal and run the system in a number of locations, have been funded by NDPCAL.

The CAMOL system is designed to perform all the CML functions listed at the beginning of the chapter. It is too soon yet to be able to give any accurate data on the overall resource requirements of running the system or even to say accurately what its development costs have been, although ICL have invested very roughly £100,000 in CAMOL. Licensing arrangements and charges which ICL will make for the system have not yet been decided, therefore it is not possible to allow for any write-off of development cost in discussing resource implications of CAMOL.

ICL believe that the system will have increasing application both at home and abroad; their marketing policy aims first to establish CAMOL in UK educational institutions and then to exploit other opportunities, including the private sector. In their view, the main impetus for the use of CAMOL will come from an increased emphasis in education on control, coordination, monitoring, and changeover between courses, together with a worsening of the staff-student ratios and hence larger class sizes. Increasing emphasis on costs in industry likewise could bring a need for greater control and monitoring in industrial training. They also foresee in the longer-term future a use for the system from an expansion in further education brought about by early retirement and more job retraining as results of a deteriorating economic climate; this would lead to high student costs and hence teachers coping with more classes in different locations with consequent problems of management control.

The National Programme has sponsored applications of CAMOL in secondary, further and higher education and in military training. The projects are based at the New University of Ulster (with applications in the Ulster College and in Methodist College, Belfast as well as in the university itself), Brighton Polytechnic, Bradford College and the 8th Signals Regiment at Catterick. In all cases NDPCAL has supported the development of the educational material by funding the development staff and has also been responsible for some enhancement of the system software, notably at Brighton where the test analysis suite of CAMOL was developed.

### 5.5 Resource implications of CML in tertiary education

All NDPCAL's investment in CML at this level is in applications of CAMOL. The largest of these projects and the one which is nearest to a steady state is in the Education Centre at the New University of Ulster (NUU). This project has been running since August 1974 and by the end of the present phase roughly £100,000 will have been invested, 80% of it by NDPCAL and the remainder by the university.

The largest part of the development effort has been put into redesigning a course on curriculum design and development which is a compulsory part of the undergraduate and certificate course in the department. It is based partly on materials produced by the Open University and partly on specially prepared material on local school-based curriculum development. The course represents a third of the students' work load for one-half of their second year. It consists of 12 multi-media resource self-study modules of which each student chooses between three and five. The material is housed in a library-based resource centre containing ten private study carrels with audio-tape replay and slide-viewing facilities, and a seminar room for group work. In the last year 175 students participated in this course for which CAMOL is now fully operational.

Although this is the only example so far of a fully computer-managed network type of course which has been specifically developed for CAMOL, there are four other courses in the department in which the system is used to varying degrees. One course, for example, on 'research design and structure' can be termed 'individualized linear' in that all students follow the same eight-week course. This is for part-time mature students who have a wide range of ability in the subject and CAMOL is used for testing, marking and providing assessment information to the tutor. The students take their study material and tests home with them and post their answers (on optically marked cards) to the university for processing; the results are available at the next weekly seminar.

Using CAMOL does have a significant effect on the allocation of staff time in the department but it is not possible to generalize. Some staff have less student contact time on CAMOL courses thus freeing them for other activities and courses. The project director or his colleagues would be expected to provide 22 hours a week on the curriculum design course if it were a conventional one, but in its CAMOL-managed form the contact time was 12 hours last year and will probably be less in the next year. This means that the project director can manage the course alone which would not be possible if it were a conventional one. The tutor for the research design and structure course on the other hand has the same contact time as previously but spends it with fewer students — those who have been selected by the system for tutorial sessions.

Overall it is unlikely that there will ever be a sufficient number of the curriculum design type of course to save staff, whose numbers will continue to be determined by general staff-student ratios. However, this application has shown that fully individualized courses with large student numbers are a practical possibility: without CAMOL it is very unlikely that the course would exist in its present form. Although no staff are saved it is possible to reduce staff commitment in selected areas, once the development phase is over, allowing them to transfer to other areas on which they wish to concentrate. In total at NUU, about 400 students are involved to some degree in CAMOL for about one-sixth of their curriculum time for the year. Past system and educational development (not including promotion, administration, teaching and evaluation), account, however, for an investment of around £30,000, most of it in the form of staff time and about two-thirds of it provided from NDPCAL funds. We estimate the steady-state cost, including running costs together with a write-off of development expenditure, to be of the order of £34 per student per year. This is an average over all the different applications so far and obviously covers a wide range of student involvement; the costs attributable to the curriculum development course will be considerably higher than the average and others will be much lower.

There is one other NDPCAL-sponsored CAMOL project in higher education which is based at Brighton Polytechnic. The nature of the application here is rather different from that in Ulster. Whereas the major development at NUU has been in an in-depth reorganization of some course units for resource-based self-teaching within one department, each involving a small number of staff but using most of CAMOL's facilities at a very micro level, the application at Brighton will involve a wider spread across departments but with little or no reorganization of the courses themselves. The emphasis is on computer test-marking and question analysis and on record keeping, with little on student routing. The first part of Brighton's work concentrated on developing the test marking and analysis suite of programs which has since been adopted as part of the general CAMOL package and which was based on a smaller program already developed and used in the Polytechnic. The complete CAMOL suite has been loaded and tested on Brighton's computer using past student data. It is planned to involve over 600 students in various applications in the 1977-78 academic year.

The most advanced application will involve nearly 200 students in the Combined Studies BSc in applied science. The first year of this course is conventionally taught but already exists in a modular form; it is run by 16 lecturers in different disciplines and presents a difficult organizational and administrative problem for the course director in maintaining records of students, including their progress through the units of the course, the results of their frequent tests on various units, their attendance records and any remedial work which may have been recommended. An earlier Brighton test-marking program was already used to some extent on this course and in the 1977-78 year the CAMOL suite will be used extensively for marking and question analysis and for record keeping. The principal benefit is expected towards the end of the session when the course director has the task of collating the records of computer-marked tests, other examinations, interviews, practical work and attendance, in order to make recommendations to the Examinations Board on each student. CAMOL it is hoped will carry out much of this analysis, including giving predetermined weights to different aspects of the testing and other assessments, in addition to producing routine reports throughout the year for students, tutors and the course director.

Several other applications are scheduled to begin in the year. Another example is a mathematics 'levelling up' course which runs through the first term of the first year for all science undergraduates. This is a service course run by the mathematics department intended to bring the students to the required level for them to understand the mathematical content of their respective main courses. It already exists in self-tuition form but will, at least for the present, continue to be mainly tutor-marked as personal contact is thought to be very important in this type of course. The students take an initial test and, on the results of this, are directed to some of a set of six self-teaching packages in various branches of mathematics. About 300 students from different subject areas and 12 tutors are involved so that once again there is a difficult administrative problem and the maintenance of student profiles by CAMOL is expected to alleviate the burden. An elementary form of routing will be employed for this course as the computer will direct students to the course units on the basis of their performance in the initial test.

Other courses will vary in their use of different CAMOL facilities, but overall the emphasis at Brighton, unlike some CML projects, is on the educational administration problem of the course directors of multi-discipline courses involving large numbers of students and staff, rather than on the development of course curricula or multi-resource learning methods. Nevertheless a significant effort is required from the academic staff in specifying questions, methods of analysis and reporting procedures. While it is obviously too soon to pronounce on resource implications, some preliminary estimates can be made. For the combined studies course the total educational development and systems work required an investment roughly of the order of £10,000 in staff time of which perhaps 25% represented marginal expenditure from the CAMOL development officer and his assistant (the remainder coming from the academic staff). The steady-state costs for the course, representing a write-off of the development cost and including operational expenses of hardware and staff, are likely to be very roughly around £30 per student. In the long term the marginal resources required to provide CAMOL facilities for the college will probably consist of a full time CAMOL officer and assistant with part-time commitment from computer staff and the educational development unit. There is also likely to be a need for computer enhancement, amounting to around £18,000, to meet CAMOL needs from 1979 onwards.

### 5.6 Resource implications of CML in secondary education

The National Programme's main investment in this area has been the Hertfordshire Computer Managed Mathematics Project. This is one of the two projects we have selected for case study presentation (see Appendix B) and consequently little detail need be given here. The project has been a major one in the development of both curriculum and systems. A complete mathematics course for the first two years of secondary level has been produced, with printed material and TV tapes; the CML system used is a 'tailor-made' one designed specifically for the course. Annual operating costs (at county level) in Hertfordshire are around £11 per pupil or £6 in marginal cost terms. If the systems and educational development were completely written off over five years and only over the 4000 pupils expected to be using the system during 1977-78, the total annual steady-state cost would be about £15 per pupil; increased use of the system by other authorities would of course spread the development cost wider and reduce the unit cost.

Another system is that developed by the London Borough of Havering, initially for use in its own schools but now being sold to other authorities. This is a content-free system and the principal courses developed for it so far are in third-year biology; two self-contained courses, one in respiration and one in photosynthesis, each providing half-a-term's work, are used extensively in Havering. The system provides marking, routing, monitoring, reporting and the allocation of apparatus for the practical work. The development was funded not by NDPCAL but by Havering itself and the Social Science Research Council. The National Programme however have funded a project to translate the Havering software into a different computer language to make it more widely available, and to test the new system in Lothian; the transfer aspects of the project are covered briefly in Chapter 7. Although the CML system itself is not NDPCAL funded some indication of costs can be given.

The computing and distribution costs for a four-school trial in Lothian Region are about 60p per pupil per week, or say £7 per pupil to cover the two courses. At present none of this is an extra cost as it is being absorbed by the existing facilities, but the costs would soon become marginal with an increase in the number of schools involved.

This figure does not include any share of the development cost of the system or educational material; the system is a large one and, like CAMOL, intended for much wider application eventually and it is not possible to make any estimate of future usage. However, an authority can buy a licence and interface to use the software system for £2775. The cost of buying sufficient educational material for both biology courses for a class of 30 pupils is about £250; Havering suggest that this could be used by say six classes in the school each year for five years, thereby serving up to 900 children in all.

Havering have estimated their own marginal operating costs for the biology courses at 33p per pupil-hour which in terms of cost per year is similar to that achieved in Lothian. If an allowance is included for a write-off of the educational (but not systems) development, the marginal cost will be in the range 35p per student-hour (based on a target population of 10,000) to 43p (based on the present 2000 pupils).

Some of the recent applications of the system at Havering are aimed at using the CML system as a direct substitution for conventional teaching in certain areas instead of being an extra. A set of material has been developed for self-tuition in computer programming and is being used at present in two ways: for sixth-form pupils who follow the course in unsupervised school periods with only occasional teacher help; and for in-service training of teachers who follow the course at home instead of attending evening lectures. The costs of these applications (roughly £10-£15 per student for a term's course of two hours a week) are of the same order as those for conventional methods, and are possibly cheaper in marginal terms.

## 5.7 Other management applications

### *5.7.1 Macro-CAMOL*

This is a development of the CAMOL system aimed at extending existing computer assistance to academic management in the areas of record keeping, producing lists and compiling statistics. The system is being pioneered at Ulster College (the Northern Ireland Polytechnic) and is based on monitoring and advisory routing of students throughout their academic careers in contrast with other implementations of CAMOL which are applied at the course element or modular level.

The system will produce action or information records for students and staff giving basic information, test and assignment scores, recommendations and progress decisions. An important part of the system will be a routing mechanism whereby students can test their proposed future programme of studies against regulations and can be guided on the availability of relevant options. The Brighton CAMOL applications have some of the characteristics of macro-CAMOL — and in fact use one of the programs developed at the Ulster College — but they are nevertheless aimed more at the course segment level. The Ulster project is still in an early stage of development and it is not yet possible to give any costing information.

*5.7.2 School timetabling*

Timetabling is a complex procedure, particularly in large comprehensive schools, and planning for an academic year may start as early as the preceding autumn. It is the increases in options and in setting which have probably had most influence in making the timetabler's task more difficult in recent years. 'Options' means timetabling a variety of subjects simultaneously so that a choice of courses may be offered, particularly in the higher forms. Considerable thought must be given at the planning stage to the available teaching resources and accommodation and to factors such as the need to combine classes in subjects where small student numbers are likely in order to justify the provision of some of the options. 'Setting' means that classes for a particular subject are timetabled simultaneously. For example, the mathematics lessons for all pupils in the fourth year of an eight-form-entry school might be timetabled to occur in the same periods for all pupils, requiring the availability of at least eight mathematics teachers as a block. The pupils would probably be grouped for these lessons according to their mathematical ability irrespective of how they were organized for other subjects.

Problems are introduced by these and other factors such as split-site schools, the availability of part-time staff, the need to spread lessons in a subject fairly evenly through the timetable cycle (which is not necessarily one of five days) or the desirability of not splitting double- or treble-period lessons. Usually the timetabler prepares a plan which he then sets out to achieve by drawing up a detailed timetable; in most cases he finds the plan to be unfeasible at many points. He may then either retrace his steps and hope for success by another route or he may recommend the lifting of a constraint or a change in the original specification of subject offerings. This procedure is repeated until eventually an acceptable solution is reached.

A number of commercially available computer packages exist to solve general timetabling problems as well as some designed by local authorities to meet their own individual needs. The National Programme has funded a project to investigate computer assisted timetabling by making a comparative evaluation of the three main commercial systems. The project has conducted special school trials and has also surveyed a large proportion of the systems' users. Much valuable experience has been amassed which will be disseminated widely. At present only tentative generalizations can be made; the project hopes, before the end of its funding period, to draw some definite conclusions from the experience gained in its comprehensive trials of the different systems.

The systems are not very easy to operate as they require some special training and usually several runs are required to achieve a usable result, with corrections, changes of the assumptions or relaxation of constraints being made after each run. Timetabling must therefore start in good time even when a computer is being used and the most frequent criticisms of the systems concerned the delays in turn-round and the 'remoteness' of the computer.

The main advantage of the computer over manual methods is its ability rapidly to run through large numbers of combinations and routes. In order for this to be done it is necessary that requirements and priorities be precisely specified for the computer methods, but this can usually be done satisfactorily with practice. The main problem appears to be in specifying the order and the degree of relaxing the constraints that the computer should follow if, as normally happens, the original specification is found to be unfeasible; it is here that the human timetabler, with his intimate knowledge of the particular problem, has the advantage.

Nevertheless, the systems are capable with some experience of considerably helping the timetabler even though generally they will not produce a complete solution. The schools varied a great deal in their reports of the timetabling effort that has been saved. Many reported no saving but a majority claimed there had been some, frequently of the order of man-weeks. The most important benefit, however, is probably in achieving a better timetable than by manual means; many schools said that the computer reports showed up the consequences of certain constraints and often allowed them to achieve a better utilization of resources or combination of subject offerings. The great majority of users were certainly in favour of continuing to use the systems. Although many of the schools reported significant savings in time, there would of course be no financial savings involved and the systems will always represent an extra cost. The charges for the two systems already used by local authorities were of the order of £8000 for an authority with 25 schools, including initial training in the use of the systems; in one case this gave the use of the program in perpetuity and in the other there are lease renewal charges after four years. Only about 200 schools are currently using one of the commercial systems in this country.

### 5.8 Conclusions

Several of the National Programme's projects have shown CML to be a practical possibility. Despite the variety of type of application and degree of involvement, there is a remarkable conformity of cost estimates, all being of the order of tens of pounds per student per year (say £10 to £40). Two other projects not discussed in this chapter, as they are still in an early stage and hence no specific cost figures could be quoted, are both using CAMOL — one for A-level physics at Methodist College, Belfast, and the other for managing the use of self-learn mathematics material for craft-level students at Bradford College. The indications are that the costs of these two projects also will probably fall within this broad range.

However, the figures quoted mostly refer to computer management of only a part of the students' curriculum and even so the resources involved in developing both the systems software and the educational material are considerable. The figures given for the CAMOL applications make no allowance for either the cost of ICL's development or alternatively for the licence fees. Similarly, those for the Havering system do not include the system development cost. As far as the production of educational material is concerned, much of the academic staff time involved in higher education can remain hidden if it does not result in extra financial outlay, although it is difficult to generalize from the few existing projects. To start up a system with the minimum extra cost would need, say, two academics giving up most of their research time for at least two years in order to carry out sufficient educational development to start a trial course. This might be more difficult to achieve in general than in a department such as that at NUU whose subject area is education and where CML development might itself be valid research, at least for a while. In the case of secondary school systems, a very much greater proportion of the total cost represents marginal outlay as there is little opportunity for the teaching staff to carry out the development. This needs to be performed by a special team which thus incurs all the cost penalties of a separate unit, not only of marginal salaries but perhaps of accommodation and services. On the other hand the secondary sector benefits from the large student numbers taking common courses within an authority and also, in principle, from the scope for transfer or sale to other authorities.

We clearly cannot quantify the benefits that are obtained from the use of CML or attempt to weigh them against the costs involved. However, in order to set the costs of CML in context it might be helpful to consider some figures for conventional education costs. In very broad terms, and based on 1974-5 figures, the total annual recurrent cost per student in higher education is about £1700; of this about £800 represents teachers' salaries and £100 books and equipment. In secondary schools the annual recurrent cost per pupil is about £350; teachers' salaries account for £250 and books and educational equipment £15, both figures covering all subjects.

Computer assisted timetabling does appear to be at least a qualified success in making worthwhile savings in the effort of timetabling, although it will not result in any staff savings and will always be on add-on financial cost. Valuable staff time is released in the majority of schools and there might also be benefits from the more efficient use of school resources although this would be difficult to prove or evaluate.

# 6. The use of CAL and CML in military training

## 6.1 Introduction

Although there are some military applications which are in higher technical and management education and are therefore similar in approach to CAL projects in universities, in general the accent in the armed services is on training rather than education. There is a great emphasis on cost effectiveness in service training and the view taken of CAL and CML is different from that in higher and secondary education in that generally the use of the computer will be accepted if it can be shown to be financially viable.

Thus CAL applications in education are often intended to deepen students' understanding of certain difficult concepts or give them the opportunity for exploring a wider range of material or data than would otherwise be possible. There is no question of shortening the course or saving teaching resources, and CAL is expected to be an add-on cost in the same way as all other educational aids, from the overhead projector to smaller class sizes. In military training, on the other hand, the objectives of the courses can frequently be clearly specified and the achievement measured by objective testing; the use of CAL or other innovations will be directed towards achieving at least the same standards with fewer resources. This might be done either by reducing the course duration, because of better training methods, or by replacing expensive or scarce instructional equipment by the computer.

There is a smiliar difference in the case of CML. In education the principal applications are directed towards solving management problems created by the new educational methods of mixed-ability teaching and modular, self-taught, resource-based or interdisciplinary courses. As with CAL, however, there will usually be a marginal financial cost to be met in return for the better information and other facilities. In military training, CML will probably be expected to at least pay for its keep, for example by reducing the number of training failures or by saving on manual methods of record keeping.

There is already a great deal of experience in the USA, much of it consisting of large-scale multi-million-dollar applications, some of which have been running for several years. However, not all of the American experience is directly applicable to Britain. The most common form of computer assistance in the US is that termed 'computer aided instruction' (CAI) in which students work interactively at terminals and follow a computerized form of programmed learning; this is an approach which is rare in the UK (although other forms of programmed learning are common). The greatest benefit of CAL in this country is believed to lie in exploiting the computer's capability for simulation, modelling and data manipulation. The UK armed forces are very different in size (a third of a million compared with the US's 2.2 million), and in structure with the British servicemen having much broader careers than their American counterparts. Thus systems that are cost-effective in America might not, in Britain, justify the heavy development costs for the much smaller throughput. In CML, many of the US applications concentrate on trainee routing in individually paced free-flow courses which are rare in the UK where almost all training uses traditional class-group instruction. The American experience, and lessons that might be drawn for the UK, are described fully by Miles (1977).

The National Development Programme has funded six significant military projects covering all three services, most of which are discussed briefly below. A useful general discussion of CAL and CML in the services, including these and other applications, is given by Miles (1977a). The military projects generally started relatively late in the Programme's life and have not at the time of writing received Final Reviews. It is therefore particularly difficult in this area to draw any conclusions on long-term financial or resource implications.

One very important feature of NDPCAL's military projects has been the good tri-service cooperation in examining the potential of CAL and CML. For example, the RAF's SAFARI project (described below) is being closely watched by the Royal Navy and the Army in preference to conducting separate projects.

## 6.2 Applications of CAL

The National Programme has sponsored a feasibility study, the SAFARI project, to investigate using the computer in technician training, and in particular the area of fault-finding and diagnosis on complex electronic equipment. Such training is carried on in all three services on a large variety of hardware, and provision of training equipment represents a considerable capital investment. Already it is impossible for reasons of finance, time and technical complexity to provide new entrants with experience on all the types of equipment they are likely to meet in their service career; this problem will become even more acute as new generations of even more complex and costly items are introduced. The aim of the SAFARI project is to investigate the use of the computer to simulate equipment faults so that the trainees can perform part of their practical work at computer terminals instead of on real equipment. To be viable, such an approach would need at least to demonstrate that there is no deterioration in the quality of training, but the principal long-term aim is to make savings in the purchase of equipment. Although the problem is relevant to all the armed services the project is based at the No 1 Radio School, RAF Locking, at which training on the Plessey Airfield Radar AR1 is given. Project SAFARI (Simulation and Fault Analysis for Radionics Instruction) is based at RAF Locking which was chosen because it already had a PRIME computer and VDU terminals with some spare capacity and the radar course in question still has a long life expectancy.

The project has been running for less than a year and a half and therefore it is not possible to comment on any long term aspects. However the basic system software has been designed together with training material for over 40 units, each representing one basic fault simulation, and the whole system has been tested on four complete courses with over 40 students and about 300 hours of terminal use. Eventual student usage should be much greater than this but at present is limited by terminal and computer processing availability.

The principal piece of software is the 'interpreter' program which controls the flow of information between the data files, the CPU and the input and output peripherals. This is 'content-free' in that it can be used with files representing any equipment with signal flow design and test points and documentation of the type used in radio and communications. New files for any other equipment would need to be created by experienced instructors typing in the information through a VDU to a prescribed format. Previously this was a lengthy process which has now been greatly simplified by the development of a 'constructor program'.

So far there has been time for only limited testing and evaluation. An internal educational evaluation is being carried out by the RAF's Research Branch which has already conducted attitude surveys of the trainees. As yet there is only limited evidence of student assessment but the overwhelming majority of trainees favoured the continuation of the

CAL system. At present the system represents a distinct add-on cost as no savings in equipment have been (or could yet be expected to be) made. The transferability of the software has recently been successfully tested by implementing it on the DEC 20 machine at Cranwell. The next phase of the work will be to run a special AR1 course in which the 'equipment time' of trainees is substantially reduced and replaced by CAL. The progress of trainees will be monitored to determine whether output standards can be maintained under these conditions.

The total cost of the project so far is about £36,000 of which roughly £25,000 is marginal expenditure. It is difficult in this relatively recent but potentially important project to gauge the long-term costs and benefits. If the project continues to be an add-on cost with no equipment saving then it will be in a similar position to most educational CAL activity where the additional cost needs to be evaluated against the claimed benefits of better learning. However, the long-term aim of a reduction in equipment cost might be achieved as a result of the RAF's reorganization of ground training which will take place over the next few years. Clearly all trainees must continue to have access to real equipment as there are several aspects of training that cannot be taught by CAL and in cases where only one piece of equipment of a certain type is made available for training purposes there can be no saving. In many cases however there is good potential for reducing the amount of equipment in the future or for dealing with an increased throughput on one location. An important demand for the SAFARI approach could be created by the new generation of more complex (and costly) equipment for which there will be no spare equipment for training. The cost implications are such that operational equipment will be used increasingly for training; however, operational needs will predominate and the scope for training will be limited and SAFARI could provide a useful supplement.

The major part of the past development, the interpreter program, is relevant to all equipment and therefore steady-state costs are very dependent upon the eventual level of use of the system. If we assumed, for the sake of illustration, that all the development to date is attributable only to the AR1 radar then our best estimate of the steady-state cost is around £10,000 a year, or £5 a student-hour. Probably a little over half of this total represents marginal expenditure with the present amount of computer usage. Figures of this order of magnitude could begin to be cost effective if the use of the computer resulted in the saving of even relatively modest pieces of equipment costing upwards of about

£50,000. This is very encouraging but there is a long way yet to go and the method still needs to be fully tested and evaluated; savings are unlikely to be achieved until after the conclusion of the ground training reorganization, which is at present concentrating on defining training content and will later consider training methods, including CAL.

The CAL project at the Royal Military College, Shrivenham, has many similarities to the higher educational CAL projects described in Chapter 4. In 1977/78 an estimated 75 students on four courses at the college will meet CAL packages in tutorial classes. While a teacher is giving a conventional tutorial, students use terminals in pairs in an adjoining room. The project has firm views on the types of terminal facility and uses a Tektronix 4010 graphic display terminal coupled to a VDU. The VDU carries messages and script so that the graphics screen is uncluttered by what are often shorthand symbols, or abbreviations. Thirteen CAL packages are available and six more are being developed. All last for less than one hour. After NDPCAL funding stops in December 1977 the project will be continued with internal resources and the department rather than the college will bear all the extra costs of CAL. As in the CUSC project, staff at Shrivenham have found that packages can help a lecture presentation, if CCTV is used to display the demonstration.

The project at the Royal Naval College, Greenwich (RNC) is based in the Department of Nuclear Science and Technology. Its aim is to assess the value of CAL for postgraduate courses at the college. The project now has five packages substantially complete and ready for trial running and evaluation, although some of them are not yet in their final forms. One package was completed before the NDPCAL project and the others were programmed by a contract software house to RNC designs. About fifty students are expected to use the material during 1978 and initially the CAL sessions will replace conventional tutorials; some extra staff (but not student) contact time will be required as two lecturers will be involved in each session with only two or three students at a time. The next phase of work after the end of NDPCAL funding will consist of trial running of the system and further development will take place if this is successful. The packages consist of simulation models of reactor systems; they are all large and students will only be expected to use part of a package in each CAL session. The material will probably also be used by RNC staff themselves for design work on reactor systems.

The project illustrates some of the difficulties in transferring complex packages between institutions. It was hoped to take over some of the Engineering Sciences Project (ESP) material from Queen Mary College, but this has not proved very successful. The main difficulties were technical ones caused by the incompatibility of different computer systems; there were also educational problems in that the package contents needed to be modified to meet the needs of RNC courses. Nevertheless two of the project's packages are based on ESP material. In one case the programme was first translated and was then substantially modified; in the other case the package was only transferred 'conceptually' in that the basic ideas were adopted but the content was rewritten and programmed afresh.

### 6.3 CML

There is potential for CML to be adopted within the armed services if its benefits can be shown to be cost-effective. The need arises particularly in the large trade training establishments with their multiplicity of courses each making use of common teaching resources of staff, space and equipment. Control of student progress and evaluation of testing procedures are time-consuming and difficult tasks in this environment and the principal requirement is for a system which will assist with the monitoring of trainee progress in the various courses, providing tutors with management information which will quickly identify, for example, potential training failures or the need for trade reallocation; there is a consequent requirement for help in the analysis of testing procedures to evaluate their effectiveness, and in the rapid production of student records so that tutors have up-to-date and comprehensive information on the courses in which they are involved.

CML has already been used to provide this sort of help on a small scale using specially written tailor-made systems. An example is the computerized quality control system using a dedicated minicomputer at the Army Apprentice College at Arborfield; this produces student profiles with the aim of identifying weaknesses early and thereby reducing training failures. The National Programme has funded one major CML project in the military sector based at the Trade Training School of the 8th Signal Regiment, Catterick. This is one of the Army's largest training establishments dealing with 14 different trades on over 60 separate courses with a total of 4000 students a year. A key activity in the School is the rigorous assessment of student performance which, as several thousand practical and theory examinations are set each year, involves considerable effort from a large number of staff. It is difficult, given the scale and complexity of the School's operations, for the existing quality control staff fully to develop and exercise the range of training validation techniques that they would wish.

The purpose of the project is to investigate the possibility of improving the quality control system by introducing CML. The project staff spent the first phase in looking at existing systems both in the US and in this country. They concluded that none was suitable for the large and complicated situation at Catterick without a prohibitive amount of development. They therefore decided to use ICL's CAMOL system and this has now been loaded and initially tested on a newly-purchased dedicated ICL 2903 computer. Some of the CAMOL facilities will not be extensively used in this application, in particular there is little requirement for the routing facilities apart from some simple remedial looping. On the other hand, the test marking and analysis routines will be intensively employed. A fairly considerable amount of systems development work has been needed to interface the CAMOL system with specially created student and test files and report production programmes which were needed to fulfil the School's particular needs.

As the system only entered its pilot testing phase of live running in the latter part of 1977 it is too early to draw conclusions on resource implications. However, the project staff believe that the cost of the computer and its operation will, in the medium to long term, be paid for by a saving of clerical and quality control staff. The initial development costs will not be recouped directly but can be set against the hoped-for later benefits. These costs amount so far to about £30,000 in staff time (of which £21,000 represents marginal expenditure), in addition to around £60,000 on hardware. If the pilot test is successful, full implementation will take place progressively from the beginning of 1979.

It is hoped that benefits will accrue partly from a saving in manpower through the computer taking over some time-consuming tasks (such as marking routine tests); partly from producing existing reports (such as individual status reports) more quickly; and partly through performing functions that are not at present undertaken (such as a full analysis of test items). A full evaluation will be made by the Army which will use quantitative measures wherever possible. Records will be kept of any saving in effort and time, annual rates of testing, reallocation, relegation and failure; surveys will be made of staff attitudes.

## 6.4 Scheduling

Another area which appears to have worthwhile potential, because of the variety of courses run at large military training establishments, is in computer assisted scheduling. This is a problem which is computationally similar to the school timetabling problem discussed in Chapter 5 but which is rather different in function as it applies at a more macro level.

Large training schools produce a year's schedule well in advance of the start of each year. In producing the schedule they start with the requirement to offer a specified number of each type of course during the year; each course will have an estimated student population and may have to be run at a certain time or may have some flexibility which is specified by giving an earliest start date and a latest finish date. As all the courses make demands on common teaching facilities such as staff, lecture rooms and laboratories and on services such as accommodation and canteens, the problem is one of scheduling the courses through the year in such a way that they all meet their time constraints without either overloading or wasting any of the resources.

The National Programme has funded feasibility studies to investigate the possibility of adapting a scheduling system developed by Oxford Systems Associates Ltd (OSA) originally for production scheduling problems which are mathematically similar to those facing the training institutions. The first study, for the Army, was terminated after the staff of the institution concerned decided that, in their view, there was insufficient evidence of potential savings and that the program, in its present state, did not meet all the constraints imposed. The second study is based at RAF Locking, and involves further development of the OSA software, but as the project has only been running for a few months it is not yet possible to make any judgement.

The application if successful will achieve its savings in two ways. Firstly, by producing a schedule of courses which is closer to the optimum than could be achieved manually, in that it produces a more even spread of resource usage through the year and hence a higher average utilization; and secondly, by the capacity easily to produce modifications to the original plan to meet changes in the requirements, which inevitably occur during the course of the year, through cancellations or additions.

## 6.5 Conclusions

There are some CAL applications in the military sector which are essentially higher education projects in nature and are thus subject to the same conclusions and qualifications as those already given in Chapter 4. The more significant approach however, in terms of long-term resource implications, is that represented by the SAFARI project at RAF Locking which set out to make significant savings in the purchase of expensive equipment by partially replacing it by computer simulation for training purposes. It is not possible at this stage to comment on the probability of the success of this aim which must await further evaluation, but the potential is there and the project has demonstrated the technical feasibility of CAL simulation for fault-finding training, and has already attracted the attention of some industrial firms.

The position is similar with regard to CML. Because of the large trainee throughput and complex organizational structure of establishments such as the Trade Training School at Catterick, there is certainly potential for the benefits that could result from better management information, but it will be some time before the CAMOL system is fully implemented and any firm conclusions can be drawn.

Similarly, in the area of computerized course scheduling, if the method can achieve any significant improvement in the utilization of training resources the saving could be very great simply because of the scale of resources involved, but there is as yet no information on which even tentative conclusions can be based. It is certainly an approach that will be pursued further and the project has already received further MOD funding. Although the termination of the Army project was disappointing as useful results might have been obtained with more time, the outcome of the Locking experiment will be at least a very valuable guide to one of the directions future work may take.

# 7. Program exchanges and transfer

### 7.1 The need for transfer

If CAL and CML materials are used only by the departments, institutions or authorities which develop them, they inevitably appear to provide high-cost methods of teaching. In most cases the educational and systems development accounts for a large part of the total cost and the most obvious way of reducing the unit cost of computer methods (that is the annual cost per student or per student hour) is to spread the development cost over a larger number of students. For this reason one of the most important aims of the National Programme from its earliest days has been to achieve the transferability of CAL and CML material developed by the individual projects.

### 7.2 The problems of transfer

The achievement of transferability is not easy as there are several factors acting against it.

— What has come to be called the 'not-made-here syndrome' or the reluctance of teachers (and not only teachers) to accept material developed elsewhere, in the design and specification of which they have had little or no say. This reluctance stems, at the individual level, from the removal of one of the most interesting facets of their work; at a national level the view is often expressed as a stand against uniformity or a desire to maintain the richness and variety of the educational system.

— There are often valid practical objections to the transfer of educational material in cases where the choice of subject matter or its treatment is inappropriate to the curriculum, teaching methods or organization of other institutions or authorities. The larger and more highly structured the material, the more valid is this objection. Thus, in principle at least, individual self-contained programs each suitable for say an hour's teaching might find acceptance more easily than a complete course of inter-related units.

— Similar problems arise because of the technical incompatibility of different computer systems. Programs written for one computer system will not generally run without modification on a different type of machine.

— Finally, although it is obviously desirable from the financial point of view that transfer should be achieved in order to reduce unit costs, there is a direct cost incurred in producing material to the standards required to ensure its transferability. In addition to perhaps developing different versions of the computer software to meet the requirements of different installations, this will typically involve printing well-prepared documentation giving theoretical background and guidance on the use of the material. Unless steps are taken to achieve an equitable financial redistribution, these extra costs of course do not fall on those likely to benefit most by the transfer. There could therefore be a disincentive to staff developing material to make their work easily transferable.

### 7.3 Methods of transfer

Transfer can be achieved:

— through formal organizations set up to disseminate CAL materials — these we refer to as program or package 'exchanges'
— by an organization which has developed material primarily for its own use selling it to others, either directly under a licensing arrangement or through a publisher or agent on a royalty basis
— by setting up projects in the first place on a multi-institutional basis — under this method all the institutions participate in the planning of the work which is then developed by individual members of the consortium but used by all
— by informal contacts which exist between workers in the same field.

This chapter deals with the transfer of actual units of systems and educational material because this is something whose effects can, in principle at least, be quantified. However, one of the most important activities of the National Programme has been to encourage the transfer of ideas. The large majority of the projects have been very active in this way, participating in conferences, seminars, 'software fairs' as well as in countless informal contacts between project staff, often involving institutions not directly concerned with the Programme. The NUU CAMOL project and Surrey University's CPTL project, for example, have devoted a considerable part of their resources to promoting the interests, respectively, of CML and CAL. The CPTL project has even transferred staff as its assistant technical director was seconded to the RAF's SAFARI project where he carried out most of the systems design and development. This secondment was, of course, costed to the RAF's project, but the bulk of the proselytizing and advisory work remains by its nature unquantifiable.

The next section discusses the different types of exchange and transfer within the context of particular NDPCAL projects. It is not possible yet to make any firm quantitative generalizations on resource usage but nevertheless some tentative conclusions can be drawn with regard to particular projects.

## 7.4 Resource considerations

### *7.4.1 Program exchanges*

The National Programme has supported two small organizations whose purpose is to exchange or disseminate CAL material. They both collect programs or packages which were not originally intended for widespread use, test and modify them where necessary, 'package' them to some extent and distribute them as requested to their members. The first to be funded was the Physical Sciences Program Exchange (PSPE) based at the Polytechnic, Wolverhampton. This covers programs in the physical sciences (mainly chemistry at present) for use at undergraduate level. The second is the Geographical Association Package Exchange (GAPE) based in the Education Department of Loughborough University and run jointly under the auspices of the Geographical Association; it deals with upper secondary level aspects of quantitative geography.

The two projects are different in their organization as well as in their subject matter and educational level. GAPE has some of the characteristics of a publishing house or professional journal in that it relies on a relatively small number of contributors of programs who are knowledgeable not only in the subject area but also in computing, and has a potentially large number of 'customers' who generally have little or no knowledge of computers and are often initially unaware of the educational value of the material being offered. The programs are 'packaged' with material giving examples of educational applications and the effect on the curriculum. The operating instructions need to be sufficiently 'robust' for the package to be used by the uninitiated (often directly by school children) with computing services provided by the local authority or a nearby college.

PSPE, on the other hand, has more of the characteristics of a club in that the members have a common purpose and about the same level of technical ability as each other. Thus most of the members of PSPE are both potential donors and receivers of material and in fact most have contributed at least one program to the library. All the members are proficient in computing, have done some CAL work and have access to a computer in their own institution.

*PSPE.* PSPE's programs are fairly small in terms of the number of coding statements. The Exchange staff fully test the programs, modify them where necessary and prepare some documentation including a statement of the purpose of the program and its theoretical basis; they then make the program available through a library catalogue to all members of PSPE. Recommendations are made to authors on program language standards but these are not always adhered to and a significant amount of the work of the staff has been modifying the programs so that they may be used on installations other than those for which they were developed.

The project is fairly computer (rather than educationally) oriented and there is no need for elaborate 'packaging' as the user is typically a university or polytechnic academic who is already using computing methods (admittedly in a limited and informal way) and can be assumed to know how he intends to use the program. He will be capable of meeting any technical problems which arise and will normally have access to a computer in his own institution. Recipients of material from PSPE often modify it, either to broaden its scope educationally or to extend the range of installations for which it is suitable; sometimes they have even translated the programs into another language.

PSPE's membership is now just over 50 which represents a fall over the last year since membership fees were increased. The number of programs requested has fluctuated widely with time, to some extent reflecting the peaks of activity in the academic year. In the last year there has been a marked increase in the number of requests for programs (despite the reduction in membership) from about 15 to 40 a month.

A considerable amount of effort has been devoted to promotion and publicity in the form of direct mailing, press advertising and holding local 'workshops', in order to increase the membership and the activity of the Exchange. Direct mailing, although expensive, has proved the most effective method of increasing membership. Currently, this is roughly equally divided between universities and polytechnics and there are 12 overseas subscribers.

It is probable that the operation could continue for some time at its present level for a marginal expenditure of about £4000 a year, using the equivalent of one full-time assistant, provided it could rely on the provision of accommodation and computing facilities from the Polytechnic or other bodies. Even with the present demand for programs this represents a cost of the order of £10 a program distributed, which seems a reasonably small sum. Although the most important benefit is probably the spread of ideas, the Exchange has obtained some information from its members which suggests that the recipients of programs estimate the resulting savings of their own programming time at about 10 hours a program. Even making no allowance for the fact that programming effort is almost always underestimated, this represents a small but worthwhile saving in terms of academic staff time.

Information from members suggests that about half of the programs distributed have been used successfully on a significant scale with students. The Exchange will become self-supporting financially if it can roughly double its present membership. The management is now concentrating on broadening the scope of activities into mathematics, engineering, physics, computer science and management studies, and believe that the target can be achieved over the next few years, in view of the likely decrease in funds for CAL development and hence the increasing attraction of pooling the resources that are available.

*GAPE.* Because of the different type of 'customer' already described above, the GAPE project has adopted a two-tier strategy for the dissemination of its packages to school level. A small central unit is responsible for soliciting, testing and amending packages and for producing a small number (probably ten) of copies of the texts and programs. The packages are distributed to a second tier consisting of a number of regional centres based on colleges, polytechnics and universities, and from them to the schools which use the material.

Such an approach has obvious advantages both financial and otherwise.

- Costs of distribution are kept low by making use of existing networks of contacts with schools and teacher groups. Costs of visits, postage, phone calls and production of package material are reduced not only for the Exchange itself but in real terms to the nation as a whole.
- The centres themselves will be likely to benefit by broadening the scope of their contacts.

— Users should benefit by having technical expertise on hand, often through organizations with which their schools already have working relations.

So far the team have had to put considerable effort into modifying programs and documentation to make them more widely acceptable but they believe that in the future as they become more established (the project has only been running for 18 months) they will be able to insist on more uniform standards from their contributors in much the same way as does a professional journal. They have also done sufficient public relations work to have already created a demand that they are having difficulty in meeting and are now concentrating on following up contacts at schools to collect information on package use, and attempting to estimate the long-term demand.

There is not yet sufficient information available for any reliable prediction of the future but nevertheless some very tentative suggestions can be made, based on the experience so far together with assumptions about the future demand. The Exchange now has 17 packages and estimates that it can build up the catalogue at the rate of say five packages a year. So far 270 copies of packages have been distributed in response to requests from 70 schools, colleges, polytechnics and universities. The project staff believe that membership can be increased by about 50 institutions a year for several years to come.

The direct costs of supplying a copy of the documentation and the program are about £2 a package and it is proposed to recover this by charging for the packages from the beginning of 1978. The fixed costs of the Exchange, covering computing, consumables, accommodation and administrative and secretarial support, are about £2000 year, mostly representing marginal expenditure; this is to be funded by the Council for Educational Technology for a limited period from January 1978. In the short-term future the project management will mainly be provided by voluntary effort and will be of the order of the equivalent of the half-time services of one academic. Thus the total fixed costs of GAPE would be roughly £5000 a year if formal longer-term arangements for staffing were made. As an illustration, if the annual demand were 500 packages (not unreasonable in view of the demand so far) the total cost involved would be about £10 a package. It seems possible therefore that the Exchange might become self-supporting financially in the longer term. However, this is likely to be a number of years away yet as to attempt to recover the full cost from the present membership would probably result in charges which would discourage use of the Exchange.

The main benefit of GAPE is in the dissemination of new approaches to the teaching of quantitative geography, rather than in the direct saving of time, as most of the users of the packages could not have developed the material themselves. Any figure for the saving of development time therefore is purely notional but it is worth noting that the project staff estimate that the development costs of packages fall in the range of £100-£400 in terms of staff time.

*7.4.2 Sales of material*

Direct sales rather than free transfer are most likely to occur in the case of large CML systems in which the developing authority has invested considerable resources. The Hertfordshire mathematics and Havering biology CML systems (discussed in more detail in Chapter 5) have both been sold to other authorities. Also the Army's Arborfield CML system (not an NDPCAL project) is offered commercially by the software house which developed the system.

One problem in transferring such large systems is likely to be the incompatibility of the software with the receiving authority's computer installation and the National Programme has funded one transfer project aimed at overcoming this difficulty in the case of the Havering CML system.

The Havering suite of programs was written several years ago in ALGOL for their Hewlett-Packard computer and hitherto this has effectively confined its sale and transfer to authorities having similar installations. The transfer project, which was a joint venture between the Havering and Lothian authorities and NDPCAL, has resulted in the system being translated into FORTRAN, successfully implemented and tested on the Lothian Interdata machine and run in live trials in four Lothian schools. The new version of the system in very much more transferable than the old one, partly because FORTRAN is a much more standardized language than ALGOL and partly because, in the new version, all machine-dependent factors have been grouped in one routine. The project also provided a valuable test of the transferability of the educational material; despite earlier doubts the Havering material was used with no real problem by the Lothian teachers. The total cost of this project was about £31,000 of which about half represented marginal expenditure. This represents a considerable saving in elapsed time and total resources compared with Lothian's alternative of redeveloping the CML system for its own use. The project has enormously increased the value of Havering's material as well as providing useful information for any future undertaking with other systems.

*7.4.3 Multi-institutional projects*

In setting up cooperative ventures such as the Computers in the Undergraduate Science Curriculum (CUSC) project, NDPCAL has been very successful in achieving the transfer of materials between the separate institutions of the projects. All the programs developed in this way have been accepted and used successfully by the cooperating members and in some cases the saving in research effort has been considerable — such as the graphics package used by all the CUSC institutions which alone took between one and two man-years to develop.

However some workers have suggested that the formal committee structure which this type of project entails does consume a significant amount of time and slows up development. Also the extra degree of refinement that both programs and documentation need in order to make them readily transferable, even within the one project, can be considerable. It has been likened to the difference between writing a set of lecture notes compared with preparing the same material for publication. One member of the CUSC project suggested that it took up to ten times as long to develop transferable material as to prepare the material for use within their own departments. Other projects suggest smaller factors but all agree that the extra effort is significant. In some cases therefore it could actually be uneconomic to 'polish' packages in order to achieve transfer on a limited scale and the eventual market for programs needs to be carefully considered by project managers.

*7.4.4 Informal transfer*

A large number of the packages developed by NPDCAL projects have been 'transferred' informally to the extent that the developing organizations have supplied copies of programs (usually a description, program listing and either punched cards or paper tape) to other workers who have asked for them. Beyond saying that the dissemination of ideas in this way is obviously beneficial it is impossible to derive any conclusions on the resource implications of informal transfer. Some projects have kept records of the number of programs they have sent out but none has received much feedback on the use of the programs; this may suggest a low level of actual usage but even this is not certain. While the cost of this sort of informal dissemination is obviously well worthwhile where programs are in fact used, it is not insignificant where 'transfer' is simply a means of spreading the gospel. The Surrey CPTL project for example has sent out about 140 copies of its CAL packages but received virtually no feedback and calculate that it has cost, in staff time alone, roughly £15 a program.

### 7.5 Conclusions

Transfer of programs, packages and systems is a key activity in reducing unit costs and this is likely to become even more important in the future. Although it is rather early to make accurate predictions, the indications from the two formal exchange schemes discussed above are favourable. It is possible that they will both eventually become financially viable and the real saving in national resources by this type of scheme is well worthwhile. Other forms of cooperation such as multi-institutional projects and informal transfer should also not be neglected, although there is a need to consider the scale of transfer and the degree of use of the material, otherwise there is a danger of the uneconomic use of scarce resources.

# 8. Value for money?

## 8.1 Introduction

The Directors of Great Britain Limited might well ask the financial evaluation agency for an account of their investment in CAL and CML. This chapter will examine the problems of measuring the results of NDPCAL, will consider whether any techniques are relevant and will review the unit costs of CAL in relative terms.

The nation has genuine grounds to be alert to the costs of new educational technologies such as CAL. Other educational technologies have been expensively installed in many universities and have not made a substantial impact in the teaching curriculum (Carnegie Commission, 1972). The portents for computer assisted learning were not good. In 1975 the UNCAL team warned 'this voraciously expensive technology is still in its infancy and has already consumed vast sums in America and several fortunes here. There is little to show for it' (UNCAL, 1975). The commercial world can show an unhappy list of American ideas which failed to cross the Atlantic effectively; might not CAL be a similar white elephant?

There are three ways in which critical questions could be asked about cost and the NDPCAL.

- Has the £2.5 million spent on the Programme been justified, compared with other national investment in the same area?
- Have the decisions of the Programme Committee and the Directorate regarding investment in particular projects been justified? Extending this, we can ask: Are some projects better value for money than others and are there some areas which should not receive further investment?
- Are CAL and CML generally cost-effective? Are they innovations which decision-makers at the institutional level should support?

Before looking at these questions we shall review the techniques which can (or cannot) help us with the answers.

## 8.2 Techniques for assessing value for money

In trying to relate the inputs to a Programme or project with the products or outputs, we usually seek a common measure for both. In industry this exists in the unit of money and a host of techniques has been devised to assess the overall net benefit over time in money terms (internal rates of return, payback periods, net present value calculations, etc). The financial conclusions are then regarded in progressive companies in the light of qualitative factors such as social and environmental impact and the effect on the labour force and job satisfaction.

Educational project appraisal rarely has a financial baseline, since educational outputs are almost wholly immeasurable and the principal effects of educational change are not often financial. We must therefore look at techniques like cost-benefit analysis and cost-effectiveness analysis to see if they can help.

Cost-benefit analysis reduces inputs and outputs to a common financial measure and then calculates a benefit-cost ratio. In the much-quoted Third London Airport study the alternative sites were each costed and all benefits were quantified (some a little controversially) to produce an order of ranking of the alternatives. Is this applicable to CAL or CML? As we have seen in Chapter 1, the results of CML and CAL projects are rarely quantifiable. The outcomes are added educational value, enhanced understanding of concepts and other qualitative products. In only a few CAL projects was there any evidence of a financial benefit. Even in CML projects the computer was often doing something that had not been done before or could not be done in any other way, so that the calculation of benefits in financial terms presented problems in all cases. We can therefore conclude that the standard cost-benefit analysis technique is not relevant to the work of the NDPCAL.

Cost-effectiveness analysis accepts the inherent incompatibility of costs and benefits and suggests that the ultimate value judgements cannot be escaped, but can be aided in many cases. In practice there are three ways in which costs and benefits can be studied.

- When projects are being compared with each other (or an innovation with that which it has replaced) the products or outputs may be assumed to be identical in both cases. Attention can then be focused on the costs of the two alternatives and the cheaper method will be chosen.
- Where the outputs of both alternatives vary, the costs or inputs of each can be held constant. The alternative which produces more benefit or value will clearly be preferred.
- Where neither costs nor outputs are constant, there is a different

problem, since we are attempting to contrast extra cost with extra value. The exercise becomes a subjective value judgement.

In NPDCAL's case every project claims that its output or product is different or an improvement; thus the first category of assessment is not applicable, since the products are never constant or identical. All projects are an extra cost overall (even after allowing for the element of replacement) so that the second category is also irrelevant. It would not be possible, given the present cost of computer technology, to adopt CAL or CML and to achieve its benefits for no extra total cost. Thus, we find that all NDPCAL's projects fall into the last of the three categories. In many cases the computer is doing something that could not be done in any other way, however, so that no comparison of any kind is possible and the judgement is whether the computer's service is worth the cost. It is immaterial whether the computer is replacing an activity or supplementing one, since in both cases there will be an overall extra cost and, presumably, a claimed added value.

In our view cost-effectiveness techniques are of little help in making the value judgement of whether an extra benefit is worth the extra cost. Cost analysis can help with the identification and measurement of costs, but cost-effectiveness has nothing to add.

Despite the absence of any clear guidance from techniques, we shall now turn to the first question we posed and consider NDPCAL.

### 8.3 Programme expenditure

The NPDCAL has spent £2.6 million under the following headings.

| | |
|---|---|
| Non-recurrent expenditure (computer, terminals) | £ 402,000 |
| Staffing costs | £1,648,000 |
| Travel and subsistence | £ 115,000 |
| Other costs | £ 423,000 |

It is estimated that the institutions themselves have invested a roughly similar sum in hardware, academic time and direct contributions to running costs. Much of this expenditure has a long life. The terminals and computers will be of continuing benefit, while staff and students may have gained knowledge or added understanding about computers and their own discipline which will never leave them.

How does this total expenditure of about £5 million over five years compare with similar educational funds? The following should help to set the total of £1 million per annum in perspective:

— Computer Board capital expenditure 1975-76 — £9.1 million
— running costs of university central computers 1973-74 — £9.4 million
— universities' expenditure on books 1973-74 — £4.67 million
— SSRC Educational Research Board awards 1975-76 — £0.32 million

Although £1 million is a substantial sum in absolute terms, it is less significant in comparison with computer expenditure and other academic services.

The other side of the value judgement about NDPCAL is based on its claimed achievements. The Secretary of State puts them boldly in the Director's *Final Report:* 'the UK can fairly claim to be a world leader . . . the historic monopoly of North America in these matters has been dented, if not broken' (Hooper, 1977). In the same report the Director becomes more specific. 'The primary product of the National Programme, on which it asks to be judged, is evidence of institutionalization' and he cites 70% as the success rate on projects institutionalized. His second aim of transferability has also been statistically successful (see Chapter 7). During the five-year period an increasing number of students have had contact with the computer. 13,380 met CML and CAL in 1976/77 and 34,400 student-terminal-hours of CAL were recorded. This is substantial, although remote from the 1,250,000 hours of instruction given by PLATO IV to 75,000 students in 1975/76 in Illinois.

Thus, we have a Programme which has considerable direct achievements and which claims to have met its prime aim against severe economic odds. In addition there are many side-benefits — a management style which is new to educational funding and which may transfer, several program languages for CAL, a mass of documentation and evaluation reports, new approaches to evaluation (both educationally and financially) and more than 700 staff with additional knowledge which could be of long-term benefit.

The NDPCAL has also some negative findings which may ultimately be its greatest legacy. It has shown that claims for large-scale replacement of teachers by CAL are unrealistic. It has identified the high costs of both CAL and CML and has scotched almost all claims for operational economies in the foreseeable future.

## 8.4 Expenditure on projects

An assessment of an individual project means contrasting the change in costs with the change in products. It is therefore concerned with the extra or net gain in both cases. Since the three levels of audience defined in Chapter 2 have very different perceptions of both costs and products (which arise at differing levels) we have to measure them at one level, the total national one.

The identification and measurement of project costs is not an exact science. We have tried to outline some of the problems in Chapters 1 and 2. As a result of these our methodology is imperfect and represents a subjective assessment of the resource impact in each case. The addition of a unit of output to the cost to make a ratio or unit cost also adds further problems. In the case of CAL projects we cannot always identify the number of hours' use of CAL materials, while for CML projects the key problem is the reduction (if any) in staff effort.

Let us, despite these difficulties, pursue an example to see how far we can go in answering the question: Is a CAL project worth it?

Our example concerns the University of Surrey's Computational Physics Teaching Laboratory (CPTL) project described in Appendix A. This has been chosen because it is well-established and the main development effort was completed some time ago.

The resource impact of the project is complex. It has required extra capital expenditure of £42,800, of which £24,100 came from NDPCAL. The development effort by staff has cost £41,000 in salary terms and of this about £14,000 was funded externally, the remainder representing time of established academic staff. Related development costs and overheads bring our assessment of the total development cost to £53,000. Each year the project's operating cost is £11,730, of which £8000 is marginal or extra as far as the university is concerned. Only £3500 however has to be provided each year from the departmental budget. Applying our standard methodology, we calculated the total national cost of the project in future as just over £5 per student-terminal-hour of instruction, while the marginal cost was much lower, until the time came to replace the computer or terminals.

The most measurable output of the project is student-terminal-hours; these number about 5500 hours a year. The project differs from many others in wishing the computer to be pervasive throughout some courses and in emphasizing that it can play flexible roles at different stages of a student's curriculum. One hour extra per week was timetabled for the CPTL and thus part of the timetabled involvement with CAL of 78 hours for each student in the first two years is replacing other activities.

Many claimed products or outcomes cannot be quantified: an improved 'marketability' of students to prospective employers, in-service training for some academic staff, addition to the department's academic reputation and the largest category of all, the purely educational benefits. These include the enhanced understanding, the increased practical experience (where packages simulate experiments), the practical knowledge of programming, and experience of the numerical algorithmic approach to problem-solving.

At each decision-making level judgements on the project would be different. The departmental level assesses the marginal cost to the departmental budget (about £3500) against all the benefits. Not surprisingly in this case the verdict is favourable. The department will continue the innovation as it already regards CAL as a fundamental part of its teaching activity. At the institutional level the value judgement is not made so explicitly, since so many of the costs are hidden until the equipment requires replacement. At this stage the institution will give considerable weight to the view of the principal beneficiary, the head of department. The focus of national concern will be on the unit costs and any comparable data on conventional teaching costs. The question may well become 'can we afford to spend £x more in unit cost terms on the claimed extra educational benefits'. In this case the focus will be on the educational claims, as the increase in cost is quantified (and small by comparison with some other CAL projects).

Our example has looked at one project in isolation and has not considered the question of the large range of costs of NDPCAL projects. Surely, an objective inquirer will say, we should seriously question the value of projects costing £20 a student-terminal-hour, when others are in the £5 to £10 range.

The range of cost in NDPCAL projects is certainly broad, but so are the range of disciplines involved and levels of educational sophistication. It would be wholly realistic to expect projects based in, for example, nuclear engineering with very expensive laboratory equipment and low student numbers to be more expensive than statistics teaching for geographers. If a CAL package replaces a laboratory experiment in a well-equipped but little used laboratory, the comparable costs could be very close.

The cost questions can therefore be refined in two directions.

- — Are any projects costing more than one would expect in the academic discipline concerned?
- — Have project directors managed the project efficiently so as to minimize costs and maximize student hours (in line with the factors listed in Section 4.1)?

It is clear that thorough answers to these questions for all projects would require both expertise in each discipline and a detailed understanding of the management decisions of each project and the context in which they were taken.

Our study of projects shows beyond all doubt that the principal factor in reducing unit costs is the number of students. The CALCHEM project provides the evidence for this. The unit cost for 1977/78 in each of the nine participating institutions for the use of the same packages with the same development cost on the same terminals varies from £5 to £15 (and beyond). The former case applies to the Open University where there is little problem in achieving 1700 student-terminal-hours in the short space of their summer schools. The upper end of the range relates to a conventional university laboratory course with all the usual problems of timetabling access to terminals in an overloaded syllabus during a short period of the year.

Student-hours should not be the sole criterion for assessing CAL projects' effectiveness and success, however. The CUSC project has achieved relatively poor numerical scores of students so far and has absorbed the largest sum of money of any project. Bald calculations of cost per student-hour in 1977/78 produce unpleasant answers. The following factors help to explain this situation.

- — CUSC has been pioneering the development of interactive graphics packages and is perhaps the most sophisticated project in the Programme. Some of its biology packages are now available in the USA through the CONDUIT exchange service.
- — The project has been consistently disturbed by non-availability of promised computer time, terminal technical problems, terminal manufacturers' ceasing production and rapidly changing graphics technology.
- — Much staff time has been spent on package development and the creation of graphics software packages in two languages for two types

of terminal. These have long-term value outside the project.

— Considerable effort has gone into investigating procedures and approaches to formative evaluation of CAL materials and the results of this work have general applicability.

The project has by no means achieved its steady state in terms of student numbers and cost per student-hour calculations at this stage are therefore unrealistic. It does nevertheless show clearly that research ventures involving technological and educational development in science subjects are expensive activities.

### 8.5 Expenditure on CAL and CML

One way of assessing CAL and CML projects is by looking at their costs compared with the existing teaching or pupil management costs. Cost studies of conventional educational activities are not numerous and have traditionally been produced as a by-product of studying the costs of new media (Layard, 1975). Following this approach, we undertook studies of the conventional costs of teaching in universities and secondary schools (Pearson, 1976; Pearson, 1977). These calculations had to be made by broad subject level and were prepared in the same manner as those from national level data. The method was broadly similar to that which we used to calculate the costs of CAL projects, with the exception of capital equipment cost which was not included in the conventional figures. Our work showed that an extra teaching session in a university would currently cost between £0.60 and £2.50 per student-hour depending on the teaching group size and the subject matter. In the secondary sector marginal costs per pupil-hour ranged from £0.22 to £0.58 according to the subject and the level.

The conclusions from our survey suggest that conventional teaching will always be cheaper than CAL, except where capital costs are a sizeable proportion of the total CAL unit cost. We can see from Table 5 in Chapter 4 that this is not usually the case, since the capital costs represent less than 25% of the total cost. Thus, the cheapest CAL project cost of £4 per student-hour is more than the upper end of the range of conventional teaching cost. In order to test the average conventional cost calculations we had made we obtained data for two undergraduate science laboratories. These showed that the conventional costs (including capital equipment, but not the development cost of laboratory experiments) were £2.6 and £3.4 per student-hour respectively. The addition of a sum for development time could bring these figures up to the lower levels of CAL costs. Taking our two approaches together, we can surmise that while conventional costs will range from £0.60 to £5.00, the cost of CAL will be between £4 and £15 per student-hour.

As regards CML, the problem was different. The computer is usually providing information and routing pupils in a way that was not possible before. In one role the computer has replaced staff time; this was in the computer marking of material (eg worksheets in Hertfordshire Mathematics Project). This computer activity should be separately identified and costed and compared with the cost of staff time on the same activity. Unfortunately the complexities and problems of doing this were too great. In one CAMOL project there was a year in which the delay in delivery of the program forced the project manager to operate a 'hand-managed' system instead of a computer managed one, but hand-management provided only part of the service required. The marginal cost of this was more than the marginal cost (to the department) of the computer system and the project had no hesitation in opting for the computerized approach. If the department were charged a wholly commercial price by ICL for the CAMOL package which reflected its development costs, the balance of cost might swing in favour of the hand-managed system, even though the benefits from it would not be so great.

As we cannot find a conventional cost of pupil management to use as a baseline for assessing CML we have looked elsewhere. The most realistic figures to use as benchmarks are the authority's capitation allowances and the annual cost per pupil. The question then becomes: Is it worth spending £6 extra per pupil per annum to help the management of four classes a week, when the annual capitation is £15 per pupil and the recurrent cost to the authority £320 per annum per pupil? (Teachers' salaries for mathematics teaching account for £22 in this latter figure.) We believe that it is too early to make an overall assessment of the value of CML since the potential of some of NPDCAL's projects has yet to be reached. The military projects in particular are claiming that overall savings will arise. Until these claims can be checked any judgements will be premature.

### 8.6 Conclusion

We have not been able to reach firm conclusions on the net value of CAL and CML, since the decisions are ultimately subjective and lie outside our expertise and our brief. We have tried to show that the same situation arises in considering individual projects and NDPCAL as a whole. Cost-effectiveness analysis cannot help greatly and solutions are only found by an immersion in the detailed balance of costs and outcomes. This raises problems of identification and measurement — on both sides of the equation. Thus, the lesson of this chapter is a negative one; that cost-effectiveness analysis cannot give the answers to value judgements, it can only ensure that the right quantitative information is correctly identified and presented. This is a vital function which in the past has often been ignored or poorly carried out.

# 9. Summary of Part B

This chapter is a summary of Part B of the report. Its purpose is to present the main points of interest and conclusions from Chapters 4 to 8 and it contains no new material. Part A has not been included; it deals with areas of more general interest and does not lend itself to a point-by-point summary.

**Chapter 4. Computer assisted learning (CAL)**

1. In CAL the computer is used for: simulating processes or experiments to increase understanding; 'drill and practice' to help mastery of routine areas; calculation and analysis to reduce tedious or time-consuming tasks; providing data storage for analytical or comparative studies.
2. Generalizations are based on the nine CAL projects funded by NDPCAL in higher education, most of which had achieved a steady state of development by 1977.
3. In the nine projects CAL was used in the syllabus in a variety of ways: to replace lectures and tutorials, to supplement classes and laboratory experiments, and to help project work or self-study and revision.
4. Precise measurement of the change has not been possible as it depends ultimately on each staff member's individual use of the CAL material. Inside one project the same package can be used in a variety of ways.
5. CAL has a small effect on student contact time. It does not normally replace conventional teaching on any significant scale and where it is wholly an addition to the timetable, this rarely exceeds one hour a week for each student.
6. Similarly, the operational use of CAL has little effect on staff time. There can be a small extra burden where CAL is an additional activity or a small saving where it is a replacement. The effect is a redistribution of the time of existing staff rather than a change in the number of staff overall.
7. A significant cost of CAL is the time taken to develop packages. This varies considerably but is normally in the range 200-400 man-hours per package.

8. Most of the development was performed by NDPCAL-funded staff. About 20-30% of these will continue to be funded by their institutions and thus there will be some continuing development from 1978 onwards but at a greatly reduced rate. Without programmer support substantial new developments will not be possible.
9. It is difficult to achieve terminal utilization much in excess of 500 hours per year. The main obstacle to increased utilization is the inflexibility of the existing timetables.
10. Total national costs of CAL range from about £4 to over £10 per student-hour.
11. CAL is nearly always more expensive, in unit cost terms, than conventional teaching. However, the marginal cost to academic departments or schools can be very low. The financial cost to a department in starting up CAL may be confined to that of the computer and terminals.
12. The cost to the institution (or local authority in school-based CAL) can also be low if use is made of under-utilized computing equipment and the time of existing staff. The impact only becomes significant when the activity expands to require extra staff, space or equipment.
13. Decisions can therefore be taken within the existing budgetary structure without an awareness of the true costs.
14. The estimated steady-state total annual costs for 1977-78 for a number of higher education projects range from about £11,000 to £43,000. Development costs usually amount to between three and five times annual operating costs and depreciation charges combined.
15. The most important element in achieving lower unit costs is increasing the number of students using the material. Others are: the choice of computing and terminal facilities, terminal utilization, choice of subject or topic area, and the involvement of academic staff.

**Chapter 5. Computer managed learning (CML)**

1. Most of NDPCAL's funding in the area of educational management has been in CML systems which aim to provide assistance at the micro level. This covers computer test marking and analysis, routing, record keeping and reporting of student performance at

the unit or module level of a course.

2. There are two approaches to developing CML systems: the general or content-free; and the particular, or content-specific, systems. A general system is expensive to develop but is aimed at a wide area of application.
3. Two large content-free systems are CAMOL, marketed by ICL, and the system offered by the London Borough of Havering. NDPCAL have funded mainly educational development for CAMOL at tertiary and secondary level and have helped to finance the transfer of the Havering system.
4. NDPCAL has funded much of the development of a content-specific system in Hertfordshire which covers two years of secondary mathematics.
5. A large amount of curriculum development often goes hand in hand with computing work so that the total development costs of a CML system can be considerable.
6. The need for CML arises mainly from the use of individualized or multi-disciplinary courses in higher education and from mixed-ability teaching at secondary level.
7. The steady-state costs of the CML projects fall in the broad range of £10-40 per student per year. This covers projects of very different natures and degrees of application and generally involves only a part of the student curriculum contact time. In the case of content-free systems the figures do not include an allowance for writing off the investment in system development.
8. A greater proportion of these costs can be hidden in higher education than in secondary as some of the development in universities and polytechnics can come from normal academic staff time.
9. The CAMOL system is also being tested for use at the macro level in record-keeping, management information and advisory routing at the course, rather than the unit, level.
10. Computer production of school timetables has also been evaluated by an NDPCAL project. Only a small proportion of schools at present use one of the systems which are commercially available. There are some problems in using the systems and in general they do not produce a complete timetable. Nevertheless users mostly find them well worthwhile in achieving a better result than manual methods or in saving some of the time of the timetabler. They

represent an extra cost to the local authority as no financial savings can be expected.

**Chapter 6. Military training**

1. Most military projects started relatively late in the lifetime of NDPCAL and therefore firm conclusions are not possible.
2. Two projects are essentially applications of CAL in higher education and are therefore subject to the general comments of Chapter 4.
3. In general, the military training approach is more cost conscious than that in education and aims to reduce the overall costs while maintaining at least the same standards of training.
4. One important CAL approach is being carried out by the RAF on behalf of all three services. It aims at partly replacing, by computer simulation, equipment which is expensive or in short supply for training purposes. It is too soon for actual savings to have been achieved but there appears to be potential in the area of technician training for communications and radar equipment.
5. The CAMOL CML system is being applied in a large Army trade training school. Live running is only just commencing but, if successful, benefits will arise from better quality control procedures. It is hoped that the system will lead to the quicker identification, for example, of student weaknesses and hence enable training failures to be reduced. The costs of the system are expected to be partly offset by a reduction in clerical labour.
6. NDPCAL has funded the adaptation of an existing scheduling package to meet the needs of the services in scheduling courses for their large training establishments. The aim is to achieve a more even utilization of resources and hence to save costs of staff, equipment and accommodation.

**Chapter 7. Program exchange and transfer**

1. CAL and CML can be expensive to develop and hence NDPCAL has encouraged the transfer and exchange of material in order to spread the development costs.
2. The main problems in achieving transfer are:
   — the reluctance of many staff to use material developed elsewhere
   — the differences in curriculum which can inhibit the transfer of educational material
   — technical incompatibility of different computer systems

— the increased cost in 'packaging' material so that it is acceptable to other users.

3. Transfer can be achieved by:
   — formal program exchange organizations
   — sales of material or licensing arrangements
   — cooperative development by a number of institutions
   — informal contacts.

4. NDPCAL has funded two formal program or package exchanges. Early indications are that each could be run for about £5000 a year and, in round figures, might be able to distribute tested and documented programs for about £10 a copy. Both need to increase considerably their membership in order to become self-supporting financially but this might be possible in the longer term. The approach appears to represent a worthwhile dissemination of ideas and saving of development effort.

5. There have been examples of sales of material by authorities which have developed their own large CML systems. NDPCAL has funded the translation of one system into a much more transportable version and the testing of the revised material in another authority. The transfer of the system software to a different make of computer and the educational material to a different county's schools were both completely successful and represented a large saving of effort compared with the cost of developing a separate system.

6. NDPCAL has funded a number of inter-institutional projects which were very successful in achieving wider use of the material they developed. However, staff suggest that it can be very much more expensive to develop material to a readily transferable stage than to prepare it simply for one's own use (estimates ranged from factors of 1.5 to 10 times). The potential benefits therefore need to be carefully considered in deciding whether to aim at full transferability.

7. NDPCAL has encouraged the informal transfer of both ideas and material and this must be an important factor in the growth of interest in CAL and CML. However, the demands on the time of staff in the pioneering institutions can be significant and much effort can be spent in obtaining feedback on material which they supply in response to informal requests.

**Chapter 8: Value for money**

1. Cost-benefit techniques are not relevant to CAL and CML whose outcomes cannot generally be quantified.
2. Cost-effectiveness analysis likewise is only of limited value as in almost every application both the costs and the outputs of the project vary. There is therefore no possibility of claiming either educational benefits while holding costs constant, or a reduction in costs while maintaining educational standards. Generally there is an add-on cost for a claimed extra benefit and overall assessment becomes an exercise in value judgement.
3. It is not possible to come to any objective conclusion in discussing the following questions. Has the expenditure on NDPCAL been justified? Do any of the individual projects particularly represent value for money? And, are CAL and CML innovations which decision-makers should support?
4. The principal achievements of NDPCAL are: the successful institutionalization of most of its projects; the transferability of both ideas and material; the introduction to CAL and CML of over 13,000 students; and other benefits such as the introduction into education of a new management style. In making a value judgement these must be set against the cost of the Programme and perhaps compared with the costs and outcomes of other examples of national expenditure.
5. Projects vary greatly in unit cost terms: some CAL applications cost less than £5 a student-hour and others over £20. However, there is also wide variation in the sophistication of the material and in the progress that has been possible towards a steady state with high levels of student involvement. It is not generally possible to compare projects with each other: they are usually aiming at different things and are at different stages of development.
6. No overall conclusion can be reached on the value for money of CAL and CML, although local value judgements must be made, taking local costs and outcomes into account. The probable range of unit costs is now known but it is not possible to quantify the outcomes, or even always to identify them. However, the evaluation has shown that it is important to ensure that systematic data are made available wherever possible, so that the necessary judgements can be made.

# APPENDICES

# Appendix A. Case study in CAL: The Computational Physics Teaching Laboratory at the University of Surrey

## 1. Introduction

With over 30 projects in the whole of the National Development Programme we do not have the resources to make a thorough appraisal of every one and normally have to be content with a broad assessment of their use of resources and potential for the future. The purpose of this study is to take a more detailed look at one project in the university sector with particular reference to the impact of the computer on the course of studies and the activities of the academic staff.

The project in the Physics Department of the University of Surrey has been chosen as it is one of the National Programme's projects which seems to be nearest to a steady state. It has been running for four years; its development work effectively finished some time ago; it is now an accepted part of the department and no fundamental change in the degree or type of use is envisaged in the medium-term future.

## 2. Description of the project

The Computational Physics Teaching Laboratory (CPTL) is housed in a dedicated room within the main departmental area. It contains ten VDUs and two teletypes connected to a Nova 840 computer. The computer (but not the terminals) is shared with another NDPCAL-sponsored project (CUSC), 60% being considered to be at the disposal of the CPTL.

The director of the NDPCAL project is the head of department who is responsible for overall policy and in fact has given considerable enthusiastic support to the laboratory and has participated in the teaching use of the CPTL as well as in the administration of the project, giving at least 5% of her time over the last four years. She is helped by:

- assistant director (academic), a member of the lecturing staff of the department who has devoted about 40% of his time to the day-to-day educational coordination of the CPTL's activities, teaching in the laboratory and developing educational material
- assistant director (technical), a full-time member of the staff of the

department in charge of their computing section, who has been responsible for the systems development of the CPTL and has given about 60% of his time to the project.

In addition to the assistant directors who are full-time permanent members of the department there are two members of the project staff who were funded by the National Programme up to the end of the 1976-7 academic year:

— a project assistant responsible for the production of documentary material, administration of meetings and conferences, dealing with the large number of visitors, maintaining records on usage of equipment and expenditure and sending requested material to other institutions
— a development officer. This post in the earlier days was mainly concerned with demonstrating in the CPTL and assisting the academic staff, particularly those with little computing experience; later, emphasis changed to an internal evaluation of the project material aimed at determining criteria for package development and, in general, to the more efficient use of the CPTL as a resource in helping to achieve the department's educational objectives.

The main aims of the project were:

— the general development and improvement of CAL materials
— the application of computing skills to problem-solving
— the production of learning packages and programs on specific topics, and the development of criteria for the selection of material
— the involvement of a large number of the academic staff and students
— cooperation with other institutions and the transfer of material
— future implementation of CAL within the department at minimum cost.

The project has succeeded in involving about 70% of the 25 teaching staff and most of the 140 undergraduate and 40 postgraduate students although the degree of involvement varies considerably among individuals. About 25 packages have been developed of a simulation type which allow the student to vary parameters in a mathematical model of a physical system in order to increase his understanding of the relationships involved. This approach is typical of the use of CAL in higher education, but this project is different from others in that it represents only a part (and probably not even the most significant part) of students' contact with the computer. The next section attempts to give more detail of the particular 'flavour' of this project.

### 3. The style of the project

The CPTL is different in its style from many other CAL projects (both within and outside the National Programme) which often tend to be characterized by:

— using the computer exclusively as a method of solving a *learning* problem
— deliberately keeping the computer remote from the student, the interface between the machine and the end-user being a sophisticated software package developed by someone else
— needing no knowledge of computing on the part of the student to whom the program is a 'black box'
— requiring a heavy investment in staff time for development, often of the order of hundreds of man-hours for an hour of presentation.

The Surrey project on the other hand is characterized by:

— often using the computer as a tool to deal directly with physical or mathematical problems
— often deliberately putting the student into direct contact with the machine in situations where he needs to write his own short program to solve the problem being investigated
— using simulation packages some of which are relatively short and uncomplicated and written in such a way that the student can often modify them to solve his particular problem. They are usually intended to be used in conjunction with a particular lecture course rather than as 'stand-alone' self-tuition packages
— having no staff specifically responsible for package development, the programs frequently being written, or at least specified, by the academic staff in their normal preparation time and typically having a development time of significantly less than 100 man-hours.

These differences have been imposed to some extent by the resources available. In the CPTL, graphics terminals (which facilitate sophisticated package construction and output) were not available and also the project is a relatively small one in staff terms by CAL standards (about £52,000 of staff time has been devoted to development over the four years and only about a quarter of this represents marginal expenditure). On the other hand the project did have a dedicated computer situated within the department which could be used as a resource with few restrictions on how or when it was employed.

Nevertheless the basic philosophy has probably changed little since the start of the project. Its main characteristic is a desire for the CPTL to become pervasive throughout the course rather than dominating in certain well-defined areas and being absent in all others. This implied the necessity, from an early stage, of involving, at least to some extent, a large proportion of the academic staff and capturing the interest of many of the students. There was a rather greater emphasis on packages in the early part of the project than there is now. While this was a result of an obvious desire to explore a new teaching medium, it was also partly due to the value of packages in demonstrating the potential of CAL to academics and students alike, and possibly also to assuage the fears of the National Programme Directorate that the project might become too computer, rather than learning, oriented.

The key to the project's perception of the role of the computer in the teaching of university physics lies in the inclusion of the words *teaching laboratory* in its choice of name. The CPTL is seen as a resource in very much the same way as is the experimental teaching laboratory. It is a resource that is generally available and whose role is diverse; it is not subject to a concentrated, structured development effort and is diffused through the curriculum; it is adaptable in different ways by staff and students to teach or investigate concepts, relationships, techniques or to solve problems of research or understanding.

The main ways in which the laboratory has been used so far are as follows:

*1. The computing course*

This is an introductory course in the first undergraduate term to teach the elements of programming. The department strongly rejects the idea that students do not need to know how to program and believes that in a numerate science subject it should be a basic part of the curriculum, if for no other reason than that it prepares the students for a later research and development environment. Pre-programmed packages can be very effective in illustrating certain difficult concepts and are used in this way within the project, but the staff suggest that even greater benefits come from the insight to be gained when students write their own programs.

*2. The mathematics course*

Part of this course is taught in the CPTL where students write short programs to carry out some fundamental operations such as integration. The technical effort itself is not great and the value of the approach comes from the fact that very careful thought is required to construct the steps in the program and this ensures a proper understanding of the principles involved. The main problem is that of the time required to introduce mathematical concepts both in the traditional way and in the numerically-based manner used in computational analysis.

*3. Numerical analysis*

A large part of this second-year course is taught in the CPTL where again students write their own programs. It is often necessary in physics, particularly in research, to solve problems to which there is no known analytical solution, and numerical analysis deals with the methods that are used to obtain sufficiently accurate numerical solutions for practical purposes. As the methods usually involve iterative procedures involving a large number of arithmetic calculations which can be tedious, time-consuming and error-prone by manual methods, the computer is a valuable resource and enables problems to be more realistic than would normally be the case in an undergraduate course.

*4. Simulation packages*

These give the student a better 'feel' for certain difficult concepts or relationships in physics by allowing him to vary the values of parameters and to study the resulting effects. A timetabled tutorial period in the CPTL is made available to the lecturer responsible for each course unit and he can, if he wishes, urge students to attend this to use a package which is particularly relevant at some point in his course. There are also periods timetabled for general CAL activity in which the student may use any of the packages for further study or revision. Relevant packages may also be recommended by a lecturer as one way of attacking a course-work assignment (perhaps as an alternative to analytical methods). The student may also use suitable packages during general free-access CPTL periods in connection with his experimental work or his second-year design study.

*5. Problem solving*

The project staff suggest that it is here that the greatest opportunities lie.

The actual skills of problem-solving are rarely taught or analysed and yet it represents a higher-level activity than the assimilation of facts. It is believed that the activity has hitherto been dominated by the mathematical methods of the calculus which has strongly influenced the way in which numerate subjects are taught. Problem-solving has relied heavily on analytical methods and numerical methods are often regarded as a sometimes necessary but 'second best' and inelegant approach. The power of modern computers is thought to be changing this attitude and the team were able to give examples of previously intractable problems being solved on the computer in ways in which provided a fresh insight into the underlying mathematical models. The 'algorithmic' methods used involve the student specifying a sequence of precise steps which eventually lead to a numerical solution. The specification of a successful algorithm is a high-level activity which requires a very clear understanding of the problem.

*6. Data handling*

Many students use the computer as a means of analysing the large amounts of data that sometimes result from their experiments in the practical laboratory. This is particularly so in the final-year project which is an important part of the course, accounting for 20% of the students' overall assessment. The project covers a genuinely realistic research problem and often involves the student in planning and carrying out a large programme of experimental work. A student using the computer in this way will often be involved in writing his own programs.

Thus the over-riding quality of the CPTL is the way in which it is diffused through the course of studies while seldom being a dominating influence. Apart from the courses on computing, mathematics and numerical analysis, which are compulsory, the student is free to a large extent to use or ignore the facility. Some students (and staff) take to it much more than others in much the same way as some are predominantly theorists while others are experimentalists. The suggestion that the CPTL occupies a similar (although as yet less generally accepted) place to that of the experimental laboratory seems a fair one. The simulation packages which students use mainly in the first part of their course are analogous to the early set-piece experiments which are not demanding in experimental technique but which bring a greater feel for the reality of physical concepts; the use of the computer in problem-solving is similar to that of experimental method where there is no pre-set approach and students must have a clear understanding of the problem to use the technology of either the computational or experimental approach; and in the final-year project both the experimental laboratory and the CPTL are resources which the student can use, singly or jointly, to tackle a real research problem.

The diversity and degree of use of the CPTL is made possible to a large extent by the fact that students are given a short course in computing at the beginning of their first year. In general the National Programme has excluded teaching *about* computers from its area of interest, defining CAL as teaching *with* computers. This particular project however justifies the inclusion of computing itself in the course of studies not only because it is a desirable skill for physicists but also because it is a necessary one in order to obtain maximum benefit from the CPTL.

## 4. Student involvement

### *4.1 Planned use*

Table A.1 shows the timetabled use of the CPTL for the physics first degree course together with periods (marked*) which involve particularly intensive free student use.

*Table A.1*

| Year | Term | | |
|---|---|---|---|
| | 1 | 2 | 3 |
| 1 | Introduction to computing | Computing and mathematics | |
| | | CAL physics packages | |
| | Computing and numerical analysis | | |
| 2 | CAL physics packages | | |
| | *Design study | | *Revision |
| 3 | *Revision | | *Project |

*Introduction to computing.* This compulsory course involves one hour per week in the CPTL together with ten hours of lectures over the term in a theatre fitted with television monitors to show the screen of a demonstration terminal linked to the computer.

*Computing and mathematics.* A compulsory course for the remaining two terms of the first year which is given completely in the CPTL and involves one hour a week for 18 weeks. (There are a further 56 hours of mathematics in the first year which are unconnected with computing).

*Computing and numerical analysis.* Again, a compulsory course which involves 20 hours in the CPTL and ten lecture-hours in the second year.

*CAL physics packages.* Students are divided into much smaller groups for tutorials than for lectures and normal physics tutorials are scheduled so that there is one for each student every other week for each course. In addition to these, periods are set aside in the CPTL and timetabled so that there is one available for each student per week. Some of these are allocated to the lecturers currently giving courses so that they can, if they wish, recommend that students attend the CPTL to use a particular package which is associated with a certain topic in the course. The lecturer, if he has the time, may attend this additional tutorial period in the CPTL to discuss the content of the package and the significance of the results. Other periods are timetabled for general CAL activity when the student may use library packages relevant to the course but where there is little or no assistance available.

*Free use.* Outside the timetabled periods the CPTL is generally available for use on a first come, first served basis. A large part of the total use occurs during these periods for:

- general revision using packages
- for the second-year design study using packages or self-programming
- course work assignments
- in connection with general laboratory work, and particularly the final year project.

Table A.2 shows the number of hours timetabled per student through the first degree course and the proportion which represents compulsory attendance.

*Table A.2*

| Term | Timetabled hours per student per term | |
|---|---|---|
| | Total | Compulsory |
| 1 | 10 | 10 |
| 2 | 20 | 10 |
| 3 | 13 | 8 |
| 4 | 15 | 10 |
| 5 | 15 | 10 |
| 6 | 5 | 0 |
| 7-9 | 0 | 0 |
| | 78 | 48 |

Taking into account the current student population in the first and second years of the course, about 95 student-hours are timetabled per week on average over the academic year, of which 58 represent compulsory units.

*4.2 Actual usage*

The use during the 1976/77 academic year by students was about 170 terminal hours per week during term time. The corresponding figure for the previous year was about 190 hours — the fall in usage is partly but not entirely accounted for by smaller first and second year student numbers. A breakdown by type of use has been supplied for one corresponding week in the second term of each year and is shown in Table A.3.

These results suggest that use during timetabled periods has fallen while free use has increased. Although not too much should be read into the actual figures which are based on small samples, the staff confirm that this has been the trend over the life of the project. The major part of the timetabled use occurs in the compulsory mathematics, computing and numerical analysis courses where attendance is around 80%. Although an hour a week is available for use with physics CAL packages, there are in practice 25 packages available over the first two years of a student's degree course, so that one would not expect even the most diligent student to use the self-tuition material for more than around half of the nominally available time.

*Table A.3*

| Terminal use (percentages) | | |
|---|---|---|
| | *1975-6* | *1976-7* |
| Timetabled | 40 | 27 |
| Free | 28 | 49 |
| Total undergraduate | 68 | 76 |
| MSc | 32 | 24 |
| Total student use | 100 | 100 |

Originally it was intended that a proportion of the normal physics tutorials be held in the CPTL to involve as many of the lecturers as possible from the start. However, many of the staff were reluctant to give up a general teaching period in order to spend the time on one specific topic using a package. It was therefore decided that an extra hour per week should be made available in the CPTL and it is this hour that is timetabled for CAL package use. At first many of the staff attempted to be present in those sessions where packages relevant to their own course were scheduled to be used.

Student attendance under this system during 1974-75 was high, averaging about 70% or around the same as for conventional tutorials. This procedure, was, however, very demanding on staff time because of the number of tutorial groups involved and it was often impossible, because of timetable commitments, for lecturers to be present at all the tutorials. The more usual practice now is for the periods to be made available for CAL package use but without academic staff in attendance in the CPTL — although a demonstrator will often be available.

The project staff have calculated that on average about 40% of students actually used CAL physics packages which were scheduled for use during timetabled periods in the last two academic years. This is probably an underestimate as it was derived from the total logged time for each package by assuming that 50 minutes of connect time represented use by one student. Some packages do not take this long to complete, particularly when the teacher is not present; also any failure of the computer logging system obviously results in a reduced attendance figure.

The average of 40% covers a range of effectively from zero to 100% of students using particular packages. The staff have analysed the use of some packages in more detail and found that attendance is high when the use of a package is directed strongly by the staff; when the package is directly relevant to the lecture course; and particularly when the lecturer is himself present in the CPTL. Some packages also have a high utilization in non-timetabled periods where they are relevant to work which counts towards the students' final assessment (course work assignments, the design study, or topics that are often set as examination questions).

*4.3 Use per student*

The overall use by undergraduates is a little over one hour per term-week on average through their course. The involvement is much higher during the first two years when all the timetabled use occurs. These timetabled periods amount to about 5% of the student's scheduled contact time; this is equivalent to about 25% of the time which is scheduled in the experimental teaching laboratory. Overall, probably between 30 and 50 hours over the first two years of the degree course represent additional timetabled commitments for each student.

## 5. Staff involvement

### *5.1 Effect on contact time*

There is a considerable effect on the contact hours of those staff in the department who teach mathematics and the associated numerical analysis and computing course. There are 144 lecture-hours timetabled in these subjects over the first two years of the first degree course of which 68 are either in the CPTL or are directly associated with the computer-related courses. These 68 hours account for 415 lecturer-contact-hours out of about 500 in total. The disproportionate demand of the computer-based courses arises mainly from the necessary division of each class into five tutorial-size groups for tuition in the CPTL and, to a lesser extent, because two lecturers attend the first-year sessions in order to broaden the computing experience of the staff themselves. There is thus some element of in-service training included in these extra contact-hours which will not continue indefinitely.

It is difficult to say exactly how much extra contact time is involved in the mathematics courses as a result of the CPTL as this depends on what the curriculum would otherwise have included. If we assume that the total student contact time has remained unchanged then this implies that the lecturer contact time has increased by about 350 hours a year. This is spread over about six members of staff but falls particularly heavily on two or three of them.

There is little effect on the contact time of the staff teaching the physics courses as there are no lecture courses held in the CPTL and few of the timetabled sessions for CAL package use are attended by the staff. The earlier practice of holding some tutorial sessions in the CPTL and scheduling them for particular packages, with the appropriate lecturers in attendance, was more heavy in its demands on staff time and was discontinued because of this and the consequent problems of timetabling. If lecturers had attended all of the timetabled CAL package sessions they would have been involved in an extra 120 hours of contact time in total over the year. In practice, only about half of this figure was ever achieved.

Most of the staff contact time in the CPTL is additional rather than a replacement, although there is some replacement in the mathematics course. When the CPTL was set up the project director said that she aimed to keep extra staff contact time to below 10% on average. As the total additional contact time is probably less than 400 hours a year for the 25 staff she has clearly succeeded in this, although of course the main burden of the extra time fell on a few of the staff whose individual contact time has increased enormously.

*5.2 Effect on other academic staff time*

Apart from the head of the department, in her capacity as project director, and the lecturer holding the post of assistant director (academic), who have been heavily involved in the administration and organization of the project, the main demand on staff time has been in the development of packages and course material. Over the whole four years of the project this has been estimated at 2% of the time of the 16 academic staff actively involved. This varies considerably between individual members of staff: the lecturer largely responsible for the numerical analysis course devoted about 25% of his time to developing the course material (and another 25% to teaching it). The involvement has decreased with time: at the mid-term evaluation of the project 11 packages had been completed and 14 were in the course of development; now 24 are completed and three being developed, while future development in the steady state is expected to be about three packages a year.

This decreasing commitment to package development was of course inevitable once the initial aim of establishing a respectable library had been achieved, but it also reflects the diminishing staff time available for this work. In the first phase of the project the team included a full-time assistant director responsible for package production and documentation which removed much of the detailed work from the academic staff. This post no longer exists and much of the work falls on the lecturers themselves, while in the future the situation will be even more acute as there might be no extra staff at all available for running the CPTL. However, the fall in the development of packages may also reflect, to some extent, a gradual change in attitudes, among both staff and students, away from pre-programmed material towards the possibilities opened up by the use of self-programming.

*5.3 Staff attitudes*

We have conducted short interviews lasting about 20 minutes each with 18 of the department's 25 academic staff in which we discussed the ways they used the CPTL, how they would like to see it develop in the future, and what they saw as its particular strong and weak points. We shall leave aside in this section the views of the head of department, her assistant director, and the lecturer who was responsible for developing the numerical analysis course, as they are largely committed to the project and are obviously enthusiastic about its value. The remaining lecturers are those with, as yet, little personal stake in the venture but, as this project depends for its future support on acceptance throughout the department to a much greater extent than is so in other similar projects, it is with these staff that the success of the CPTL must lie.

All of the staff to whom we spoke seemed genuinely to accept that the CPTL is now an integral part of the department and none wanted to reduce its overall activity. This though was about the limit of unanimity in their views which otherwise covered a wide range of opinion and it is not easy to summarize their comments in any systematic way.

Not surprisingly, the best discriminator of their opinions on the value of the CPTL was the level of computing expertise of the individual members of the department. There were five lecturers with little or no computing experience. One of these could be called a 'middle of the road' man: he was quite enthusiastic about self-tuition packages with a good appreciation of their value and would like to become more involved personally; he saw the CPTL as making a small but significant contribution to the educational achievement of the department. The remaining four in this group represented the least enthusiastic end of the spectrum of opinion, although even here there was only one who was prepared to dismiss the project entirely — certainly as far as his own involvement was concerned. This whole group of non-computer men tended to view the CPTL almost entirely through the medium of packages which in general they thought a nice idea but they were, in varying degrees, critical of the achievement in what seemed to some of them to be narrow subject areas. Three expressed fears that students might devote too much time to using computer models and stressed the value of conventional teaching methods, while two commented on the excessive demands on their time if they were to become more actively involved. Only one mentioned the value to physics students of learning something of computing as a help in their future careers.

There were nine lecturers who were at least moderately proficient in computing; some of them were very expert having used computers for years while others had only come to it recently through the CPTL itself. This group was, without exception but in varying degrees, enthusiastic about the presence in the department of the CPTL, many of them voicing the identical sentiment that they now 'couldn't imagine the place without it'. Interestingly, none of them wanted a significant expansion of activities which they all thought to be at about the right level. A majority mentioned that graphics terminals would be an attractive enhancement, but they mostly thought it would be difficult to justify the expenditure.

However, despite their general agreement in welcoming the CPTL these lecturers differed significantly among themselves in their perception of its role in the department's activities. As a group they looked on the computer in a much broader way than the non-computing staff, laying much less emphasis on pre-programmed packages. Only two could be classed as unreservedly enthusiastic about the CAL package approach and two more appreciated their value but had little personal involvement with them. Four voluntarily expressed reservations about the value of packages and the same number (although not the identical set) were concerned about the time required to develop pre-programmed material. Six thought the computer a very valuable tool for data handling in the analysis of experimental results, and three for the tabulation of numerical values of complex mathematical functions, while four thought it particularly beneficial in introducing students to computers. Two lecturers praised particular packages which allowed students to simulate the repetition of experiments a large number of times with random changes in certain parameters in order to demonstrate results which depend on statistical replication, the emphasis being on the saving of time and money rather than on directly obtaining a better understanding of physical principles.

There was thus a tendency among a number of this group to give weight to the computational rather than the teaching aspects of the CPTL, one saying he saw it purely as a tool (although a valuable one) and not as an educational venture at all. However, this view was balanced by five of the staff talking of the insight that could be obtained by using models which allowed the students to vary parameters. Several of them mentioned the educational benefits of students writing their own short programs (one of them thinking the work should be exclusively of this type), and three specifically raised the subject of the algorithmic approach to problem-solving as a valuable educational activity.

## 6. Costs and resources

### *6.1 Expenditure*

The expenditure of the project is broken down below under the three headings of capital, development and running costs. The capital costs are those actually incurred by the project over its life; the development costs are the project team's estimates of the total project expenditure attributable to both educational and systems development; and the running costs are their estimate of those currently obtaining in the final phase of the NDP funded period, and which they would expect to continue in the future if sufficient funds are available.

*Capital costs*

| | |
|---|---|
| Computer (60% of purchase price) | 32,600 |
| Terminals | 10,200 |
| | £42,800 |

This all represents marginal or avoidable expenditure, £18,700 provided by the university and £24,100 by the National Programme.

60% of the cost of the computer is attributable to the CPTL, and the remainder to another NDP project in the university.

*Development costs*

| | | | |
|---|---|---|---|
| Institutional staff time: | Director, 7½% | 2,000 | |
| | Assistant director (academic), 39% | 9,200 | |
| | Assistant director (technical), 57% | 10,400 | |
| | Teaching staff | 6,200 | |
| | Programming staff | 150 | |
| | | | 27,950 |
| NDPCAL - funded staff: | Technical author | 5,500 | |
| (all for part of the project only) | Demonstrator | 1,600 | |
| | Development officer | 3,900 | |

| | | | |
|---|---|---|---|
| | Administrative assistant | 2,500 | |
| | | | 13,500 |
| Other costs: | part of earlier or associated projects | 3,500 | |
| | institutional overheads | 8,000 | 11,500 |
| | | | £52,950 |

Of this £53,000 total, about £15,000 represents marginal expenditure, all of it funded by the National Programme. The contribution from the department by way of the time of its existing permanent staff is of the order of £30,000 and from the university in the form of a share of overheads, £8000.

*Annual operating costs*

| | | | |
|---|---|---|---|
| Equipment and consumables: | computer maintenance | 2,400 | |
| | terminal maintenance | 1,000 | |
| | consumables/ documents | 600 | |
| | laboratory space | 1,300 | |
| | overheads | 1,000 | |
| | | | 6,300 |
| Staff time: | Demonstrator | 400 | |
| (all for part of their time) | Development officer | 1,900 | |
| | Administrative assistant | 1,600 | |
| | Teaching staff | 1,530 | |
| | | | 5,430 |
| | | | £11,730 |

Of this total, nearly £8000 represents marginal expenditure, about equally divided between the departmental budget and the National Programme. The remainder is made up of a notional university contribution through space and overheads, and the departmental staff time in teaching contact hours (most of it arising from the mathematics, computing and numerical analysis courses).

*6.2 National annual cost*

For the purpose of producing a standard comparison between different projects we usually calculate a steady-state annual cost which includes:

— the computer capital cost depreciated over seven years
— peripheral equipment cost depreciated over five years
— a write-off of the development expenditure over five years
— the latest cost available for the annual operating expenditure.

Treating the costs given in section 6.1 in this way we obtain:

| *Annual costs* | |
|---|---|
| Capital | 6,700 |
| Development | 10,590 |
| Operating | 11,730 |
| | £29,020 |

This method assumes that the whole of the development expenditure will be incurred on average every five years indefinitely; for a project which has been in the development phase for four years, this might over-estimate the costs as it implies that the past level of development activity will continue virtually unabated. The project staff feel that the CPTL is already in a steady state and that future development will require little specialist effort and will continue at a lower level than in the past in very much the same way as new work is introduced into the practical teaching laboratory. On the other hand, CAL is still a very new method of teaching and packages will probably become outdated more quickly than experimental procedures so that another phase of development effort might become necessary in a few years' time.

Also the operating costs for the steady-state future are a little uncertain as the figures given above assume that some other source of funding is found to replace the National Programme-funded share of the development officer and administrative assistant. If the department is not successful in this aim then the costs will be correspondingly reduced although some of the project's activities, particularly evaluation and outside contacts, will suffer. Overall, the figure of about £29,000 a year can probably be regarded as an upper limit.

Of this total, about £17,600 a year represents marginal expenditure. This is made up of £6700 for equipment replacement, £3000 for further development and £7900 for operating.

### 6.3 *Costs at the department and institution level*

Marginal costs at the department level are low, amounting to about £4000 a year for equipment maintenance and consumables. However, the development of the project represents a notional contribution of £30,000 from the department in staff salaries and a very real effort in terms of the time of the staff involved. The largest part of this contribution is represented by the time of the two assistant project directors which totals about four man-years of effort.

In addition to the departmental expenditure, the institution has contributed £18,700 of marginal funds in the form of capital purchases. The other institutional provision is in the form of accommodation and general services which represents a notional expenditure of around £2000 a year, little of which represents marginal spending.

### 6.4 *Terminal utilization and unit costs*

Each of the ten terminals is used for about 20 hours a week which represents a utilization of around 30%.

Students use the terminals for about 5500 hours a year (550 hours per terminal per annum). The full national annual costs given in section 6.2 are thus equivalent to £5.3 per terminal-hour. (The students work mostly alone and therefore a terminal-hour is roughly equivalent to a student-hour). The marginal cost is equivalent to £3.2 per terminal-hour.

In terms of annual cost per student, the corresponding figures are £185 for the total national cost and £110 for the marginal cost.

### 6.5 *Costs of the experimental teaching laboratory*

As the CPTL has been likened to the experimental laboratory in many ways it is interesting to compare their unit costs. Some approximate costs for the undergraduate experimental laboratory have been supplied by the project:

| | |
|---|---|
| Equipment (7-year life) | 6,300 |
| Space (at £2 per sq ft) | 9,600 |
| Maintenance | 2,500 |
| Services and sundries | 1,400 |
| Technical staff | 10,000 |
| Demonstrators | 1,200 |
| | £31,000 pa |

Assuming 12,000 hours of student use a year, this gives a cost per student hour of £2.6. The cost components used here are comparable with those used in calculating the steady-state cost for the CPTL of £5.3 per terminal-hour, except that the cost for the experimental laboratory includes no allowance for educational development on the part of the academic staff and to this extent will be an underestimate. In the case of the CPTL, development costs represent about a third of the total cost.

# Appendix B. Case study in CML: The Hertfordshire Computer Managed Mathematics Project

## 1. Introduction

NDPCAL has only financed one major CML project in secondary education. Although funds have gone to projects in Havering and South Glamorgan for CML activities, the Hatfield Mathematics Project (HCMMP) is the only continuing CML project with external finance wholly from NDPCAL. It therefore deserves some attention.

Like many other NDPCAL projects it is a unique operation. It would not claim to be a purely CML project since it mixes with several other educational and media innovations, which makes an independent evaluation of the CML component extremely complex. It would therefore be unwise for a reader to draw too many generalizations about CML as a whole from this case study.

CML has been defined by Richard Hooper as fulfilling one or several of the three functions of testing, prescribing or routing and recording. A fourth role of reporting on students' results is thought very important by the project. HCMMP would never claim great sophistication in its routing or prescription, although it would suggest that it had now overcome most of the technical problems of computer marking worksheets and recording pupils' results.

## 2. Description of the project

The project was one of the first commissioned by NDPCAL in 1973. Its base has been the Advisory Unit for Computer Based Education in Hatfield, one of the pioneers in exploring the application of computers in schools. The start of the project coincided with the Education Authority's decision to introduce comprehensive education and the adoption of mixed ability teaching in some mathematics classes. This presented some teachers with immediate problems: how should they organize their material? Should they necessarily adopt a pupil-centred approach to their work? How much development effort would be required to modify their present teaching method? How did they retain control of a class of 30 each doing different tasks?

The HCMMP provided possible solutions to most of these problems and thus its arrival was fortuitous; indeed the conjunction of problem and partial solution led some enthusiasts to proclaim that mixed ability teaching with a full degree of individualized learning was not possible without CML.

The project provides teachers with a complete set of multi-media teaching materials for the first- and second-year mathematics classes in secondary schools. Once in the project a teacher will receive twelve 'modules' or topic packages for the first-year and thirteen for the second-year course. Each module is intended to provide instruction for pupils for three weeks. A typical module is number 3 called 'Fractions, part I'. This includes:

— a set of teachers' notes in a booklet which describes the objectives, gives subject notes and other information and provides answers to worksheets for pupils
— study sheets for the children which summarize information on the topic
— worksheets which teach and test the topic at various levels of difficulty
— two special sheets for pupils to use in games and exercises — a sheet of domino cards and one 'equivalent fraction sheet'
— a videotape of a programme made by the Hertfordshire Educational TV Centre, which introduces the pupils to the topic and which often features the staff of the HCMMP.

The teacher may take just the material and decide not to use the CML system at all. If he does he will find that, because the course is worksheet-based, he will be doing much more marking than usual. He will also find that he is having to spend time organizing worksheets and tasks for each pupil in class.

If however the teacher takes full advantage of the HCMMP system (and almost all do), he will be offered the facilities of SAM and ESYMRK. SAM, or as it has now become SAM/SAL, is a series of individual computer-generated diagnostic tests in basic arithmetic. In 1977 a new SAM course was begun with more than 100 standards; it may eventually have as many as 1000 standards. ESYMRK is a computerized marking facility for the worksheets which produces reports for teachers and pupils and records results cumulatively in registers, which teachers can ask for when they wish. The mechanics of operating ESYMRK are different between schools since two with computer terminals are investigating the practical problems of regular data input in this way.

— Two schools feed in the pupils' test entries by a remote job entry terminal using a Post Office line. The computer in the Hatfield Polytechnic Computer Centre processes the data and produces printed output and reports. These are delivered to the schools by courier van. All this is done overnight, so that teachers can always have the marked results of a worksheet the following day.
— Nine schools are served entirely by the courier system. Pupils transfer answers from their worksheets to special OMR documents (optical mark recognition). The sheets are taken by van from the school to the Computer Centre where a document reader produces a paper tape from the worksheets. This tape then goes to the computer centre and is processed overnight. Delivery to the schools takes place the following morning by the courier van.

The latter method had considerable technical teething problems, but the project staff have successfully overcome these as the rejection rate for documents is now 2.6% (1.3 due to machine error and 1.3 to marking error). On average 840 documents were processed each night during March 1977. In 1976 the rejection rate was as high as 8.5%. On the data processed via the terminal the current rejection rate for 300 pupil inputs per night is even less than for the document reader.

The syllabus content of the modules is not claimed to be wholly 'new mathematics'. It has been designed by teachers in the participating schools and the project staff and is described as 'reflecting many of the changes in teaching in the last decade', while also including many of the more traditional topics. Teachers are free to pick and choose from the HCMMP material and it is clear that many are making good use of this flexibility. Some have rewritten or adapted the worksheets and some, as we shall see later, jump in and out of the HCMMP syllabus.

The project began in 1971 in one school. When NDPCAL funding started in 1973 there was an extension to four schools and in 1974 a further four joined in the project. Finally in 1976/77 12 Hertfordshire schools were participating. Other authorities became interested during the latter year and three schools in the ILEA and one in Bolton have taken over HCMMP modules and are using them.

Statistics on pupil numbers show the same gradual increase so that by 1976/77 the usage in 12 Hertfordshire schools was:

— 3180 pupils in 108 mathematics classes
— by 77 teachers
— who generated 4200 documents per week
— from 5 or 6 35-minute periods each week in most of the schools (two schools had three and four one-hour periods).

The ILEA schools are expected to add a further 500 pupils as users of the system in 1977/78.

The staffing required to develop the project has been substantial and one of the future concerns is that a continuing central staff will always be required to administer and modify the completed system. Whereas innovation and development can often be 'financed' internally in tertiary education from research time, there is little slack in secondary education, so that major development becomes a visible extra. This is particularly true of any innovation with a technological content. During the period of NDPCAL funding the project estimates that the following proportion of its staff time has been devoted to development activities.

| | |
|---|---|
| Project director | 16% (out of 33% for 4 years) |
| Project manager | 61% (out of 100% for 4 years) |
| Course editor | 82% (out of 100% for 3½ years) |
| Educational analyst | 76% (out of 100% for 3⅓ years) |
| Administrative assistant | 49% (out of 100% for 4 years) |
| Secretary | 78% (out 80% for 4 years) |
| Programmer | 95% (out of 100% for 1 year) |
| Seconded teacher | 77% (out of 100% for 2/3 years) |

It will be seen what an investment in staff time has been required to develop the HCMMP material during the term of the NDP funding. Some effort has been omitted from the above. This is:

— the development time prior to NDP in 1971 and 1972
— the time invested by teachers in their regular liaison and development meetings with project staff — the project has always taken pains to ensure that the educational content of worksheets and TV programmes was developed jointly with teachers rather than centrally imposed by the project staff

— time spent by staff in post in Hertfordshire in the Educational TV Centre and Hatfield Polytechnic. The services of technical and academic staff were given to the project at no cost to NDPCAL (or marginal cost to the authority).

The project staff were established in the Advisory Unit for Computer Based Education in Hatfield and shared some of their facilities. The Project Director was also the Director of the Unit and could thus give only part of his time to the project; much of this was devoted to discussions and negotiations at county level about the funding of the project in the future.

The greater part of the effort of the four full-time staff members has gone into activities not directly related to the computer. These have included:

— the development and revision (with teachers' help) of all the teachers' notes, study sheets and worksheets
— the initiation and creation (and later revision) of the TV programmes for each module with the help of the studio staff of the TV centre
— the evaluation of the effectiveness of the HCMMP materials as a whole in the classroom.

Clearly, the SAM and ESYMRK programs are the key to the whole project and without them all the other development effort would have been wasted. The converse is not necessarily true since it might be possible to use CML packages such as ESYMRK without simultaneously developing from nothing a whole range of worksheets and video tapes. Thus, the heavy investment of time in HCMMP should not be taken as a prerequisite for all CML exercises in secondary schools, although the project staff believe that no CML development can be successful without a corresponding educational development.

### 3. The operation of HCMMP

The project staff and the external educational evaluation (Professor David Jenkins, NUU Coleraine) have taken very substantial pains to identify what was happening in the classroom as a result of HCMMP. As well as the regular feedback from weekly meetings, participating teachers were expected to send in reports and comments on individual modules. Staff and students from the Balls Park College of Education observed classroom sessions and attempted to analyse the kind of class teaching associated with the project. Mrs Win Knight, the educational analyst on the project staff, visited schools frequently and sought the views of teachers who were and were not using HCMMP as well as of heads, parents, pupils and the county advisory service. A wealth of educational data has resulted.

The key claim of the project was laid out in its promotional booklet, 'What is HCMMP?'. 'The aim of the project is to help the teacher in the classroom, not to supplant him. By and large, what the computer does is to free the teacher from the drudgery of marking and leave him fresh to put his energies into more rewarding classroom work'. Since this claim is the main justification, in resource terms, for the project both external evaluations have sought to investigate it fully. Knight and Jenkins surveyed five teachers in one school and asked them whether, now that they used HCMMP, the time they spent on various activities was more, the same or less than before. The answers were:

— four spent the same time on lesson preparation
— three spent the same on marking, two less
— all spent less on duplication and typing of worksheets
— three used less secretarial help
— all spent the same time organizing materials and recording the results of children's work.

There is a methodological problem in assessing attitudinal changes on the project. Most teachers will be comparing HCMMP and mixed-ability teaching with teaching in more traditional fashion. It is well known that the amount of management required in a traditional teaching session is a lot less than with an individualized approach in mixed-ability teaching. Thus, when teachers say that with HCMMP they spend the same amount of time on marking or administration, the project may well have achieved its objective of lessening the heavy burden of the individualized approach. Strict comparisons of time spent before and after the project may not therefore be comparing like with like.

Despite this difficulty we undertook a further survey because we wished to know teachers' opinions on the change, as they would see a causal link between these changes and HCMMP.

In the spring of 1977 we asked all 76 participating teachers to complete a questionnaire. 60% or 45 replied. We tried to ascertain the effect on time outside as well as inside the classroom. Two-thirds of the respondents thought that HCMMP had affected their time outside the classroom. When we analysed this further we found less unanimity, since 19 considered their working time had been reduced, while 12 either thought it the same or increased. We then attempted to identify the change by asking what they now did that they did not do before. The answers covered three categories of work:

— more administration and organization of worksheets and printouts which have to be separated and distributed
— more checks on the computer output
— more time for individual teaching, more marking after each session and preparation of supplementary (home-made) worksheets.

There was a greater agreement about the tasks which they now did less of. 20 considered they needed to spend less time preparing for lessons, 14 said they spent less time marking individual work and five found their class teaching time was reduced.

One set of questions asked teachers to describe the change in the way they allocated their time during a lesson. This has no resource implications, but is clearly a significant educational outcome. Predictably the answers varied but tended to the common conclusion that the pattern of priorities and actions had changed. A typical answer was as follows:

| | Minutes of class time | |
|---|---|---|
| | with HCMMP | without HCMMP |
| 1. Administrative work | 8 | 3 |
| 2. Some marking | 2 | 7 |
| 3. Class teaching | 10 | 15 |
| 4. Individual tuition | 15 | 10 |

Although a wide range of teaching styles became apparent from the answers it was clear that the HCMMP allowed more emphasis to be given to individual tuition as opposed to class teaching compared with non-HCMMP classes.

We invited open-ended statements on the advantages and disadvantages of the project. Answers ranged from the moderately enthusiastic to the strongly critical. We quote below some of these extremes, since they show the difficulty in separating judgements on the CML innovation from the remainder of the projects' materials and on

CML from the concept of all-ability teaching. Quoted benefits of the project have included the following statements.

— 'A constant supply of excellently prepared, interesting, varied and relevant worksheets prepared by experts. The novelty also brings instant interest.'
— 'I support HCMMP because I know that it enables me to teach a mixed-ability first-year maths class and make satisfactory progress with all levels of ability.'
— 'Much more work is marked than could reasonably be done by a teacher alone.'
— 'It enables each pupil to work at his own speed.'
— 'Most of the children like it.'

When citing the disadvantages, many teachers' criticisms were on practical, technical grounds. They complained about the computer errors, the time taken to distribute worksheets, organize sheets, cards, papers, etc, and a resulting loss in personal contact. The most common educational criticism relates to the extremes of ability at the top and bottom of the ability ranges, since several teachers thought the materials failed to cope with their requirements. An extract from one response sums up some of the more recurring critical comments.

'My time load is very different because of HCMMP. The marking task is the same as for non-HCMMP classes. Homework has to be set up to reinforce the worksheets and extend the topic. Young children do not absorb the "meat" from the sheets, often have difficulty in reading and understanding the questions. Computer print-out sheets have to be sorted between teachers, cut up to give to the pupils, often at short notice before lessons, particularly if delivery from the centre has been delayed. History sheets have to be studied generally for detailed content. ESYMRK sheets have to be collected, corrected, recorded, put into dockets and despatched in time — and all this every day. I now do all that I did before plus additional tasks dictated by the deficiencies of the HCMMP.'

The project has been very alert to these criticisms and has been actively working to improve the service it provides to teachers. It has always held regular meetings with staff and has encouraged them to make independent assessments of the balance of advantage of joining HCMMP.

In the four years only two schools have left the project, each after trying it for one year. The most recent school to leave, St Angela's was not all-ability in its classes and in the project's view preferred a teacher-centred approach to instruction. The other schools remaining in the project use HCMMP materials in a variety of ways. One school, for example, uses it in the first year only and will develop its own syllabus for the second year. Another will take the whole two courses unamended, but hopes to cut costs by re-using the worksheets. A third will take all but two modules and may break classes into ability sets in the second year. Another has made use of the project materials voluntary in the second year and has adopted them into its own syllabus.

## 4. The project in 1977/8 after NDPCAL

The participating schools in Hertfordshire have, with only the one exception already mentioned, agreed to continue using HCMMP's services in 1977/78. The Education Committee of the Council undertook to finance HCMMP for at least one year from September 1977 and the following future staffing level was agreed.

Project manager (partly on future development work)

Seconded teacher (wholly on future development work)

½ part-time administrative assistant

½ part-time secretary

Share of van driver

Document reader operator (part may be established elsewhere in authority)

Future plans envisage a continuing development and redesign of the existing material. Attention is also to be given to practical issues of further expansion in numbers, since soon the limitations of the courier van's circuit, overnight handling time and available computer power and time could begin to show. Further work will therefore be done on studying remote job entry systems through OMR cards.

## 5. Resources and costs

HCMMP has been a medium-sized project in NDPCAL's terms. It has absorbed about £142,000 of national funding, while financial backing from the county (mostly 'hidden' costs) has amounted to at least £70,000. We will now consider these bald figures in greater detail at three relevant levels of decision making.

We shall first consider the cost to a school which in practice is almost identical to the cost to the mathematics department. Teachers are expected to pay 75 pence per pupil per annum for the HCMMP study sheets and worksheets. This must come from their slender cash budgets even though home-made worksheets would in most cases have been made with paper drawn free from the school stationery store. The project suggests that in many cases the worksheets and materials are replacing textbooks, which cost an average of 50 pence per pupil per annum. Where this is the case, the net cost of 25 pence would be taken.

Other costs might fall on the school, but they are all hidden. For example:

— storage space in the classroom (cupboards and wire baskets for HCMMP papers and materials)
— staff attendance at project meetings on Tuesday afternoons, equivalent to one-eighth of the time of one person intermittently involved in evaluation activities
— travel costs to the project meetings.

We therefore find that in common with many other educational innovations the costs of the exercise do not apply at the same level as the benefits. All the advantages of HCMMP are found in the schools, yet the marginal cost of the project to them is almost negligible.

At the level of the local authority real costs emerge. We shall consider these for the year 1977/78 in two categories, capital costs, and operating or running costs.

*Capital costs*

In the following calculations assumptions have been made by the Project about the future shared use of some capital equipment which are not true at this moment. Costs of the computer are given in the operating cost section, since at present computer time is used on a large machine and their internal charging rate is used. The calculations are made for 3000 children in 10 schools on the assumption that all schools are using the batch service with a courier van.

| | | | |
|---|---|---|---|
| 10 videotape recorders at £400 each | | | |
| Shared use by project depreciated over 10 years | | 40 | |
| 1 document reader at £8500 | | | |
| Depreciated over 10 years | | 850 | |
| 1 courier van at £2000 | | | |
| Half used by project. Depreciated over 5 years | | 200 | |
| Videotape costs £159 per course (project's estimate) | | | |
| Depreciated over 5 years | | 310 | |
| Annual 'capital cost' | | | £ 1,400 |

| | | | |
|---|---|---|---|
| *Running or operating costs 1977/78* | | | |
| Central project staff salaries | | 18,600 | |
| Equipment maintenance costs: | | | |
| videotape recorders | 20 | | |
| document reader | 1500 | | |
| van (incl petrol) | 560 | | |
| | | 2,080 | |
| Stationery, cards, etc: | | | |
| ESYMRK documents | 1800 | | |
| SAM documents | 1000 | | |
| Paper tape | 200 | | |
| Other printed notes | 100 | | |
| | | 3,100 | |
| Computer time: | | | |
| Internal charges passed on | | 8,000 | |
| Notional rent and rates | | 600 | |
| Electricity, telephone, postage, etc | | 620 | |
| Travelling and subsistence | | 400 | |
| Annual running cost | | | £33,400 |

Some of the above costs are marginal or extra as far as the authority is concerned and some are either hidden or represent charges from one internal cost centre to another. We can best consider the net impact of the project on the county by asking what would be saved each year if it was to stop. This is not always easy to identify, but an approximate answer to this question is £19,000 made up as follows:

| | | |
|---|---|---|
| Some staff salaries (whole posts only) | say 12,000 | |
| Equipment maintenance | 2,080 | |
| Stationery, cards, etc | 3,100 | |
| Some of the computer costs | say 500 | |
| Electricity, telephone, etc | 620 | |
| Travelling and subsistence | 400 | |
| | £18,700 | say£19,000 |

*Total cost*

The third level of decision-making is the national level and here we have used a total cost definition which includes an element in respect of development costs. The project clearly has invested a great amount of effort in developing its modules to date and has managed to obtain funding to continue improving and developing its material. Although it suggests that a continual development is not necessary, it is certainly desirable.

The project staff suggest that the financial cost of past development amounts to £125,000, comprised as follows:

| | |
|---|---|
| Staff time, as outlined earlier | 77,000 |
| Computer consultancy | 6,400 |
| Computer time | 4,250 |
| Production cost — video programmes | 16,250 |
| Printing costs — developmental element | 4,000 |
| Hardware use for development purposes | 4,000 |
| Teachers' time at meetings | 7,600 |
| Documents — developmental proportion | 4,000 |
| Other costs | 1,500 |
| | £125,000 |

The significance of this figure is that the project estimates that £125,000 was expended in the years 1973-77 for future benefit. The year in which the time or money was spent did not benefit from the effort which bore fruit only in the following and later years. The project admits that at least one year's developmental work was wrongly designed and in the long run produced little; to offset this however a certain amount of developmental effort preceded the appearance of the National Programme. A development cost of £8000 is suggested for this by the project.

In calculating the total cost it is necessary to make what must regrettably be an arbitrary assumption about the life or duration of project materials. For how long will HCMMP materials benefit the schools in Hertfordshire? We have chosen a standard five-year depreciation period for all projects in the NDPCAL. Following this assumption, our calculation of the national total cost in 1977/78 of the HCMMP becomes:

| | |
|---|---:|
| One year's share of development cost | 25,000 |
| Capital cost | 1,400 |
| Operating costs | 33,400 |
| | £59,800 |

In 1977/78 we understand that about 4000 pupils will be using the HCMMP system nationwide; the cost per pupil would in theory be about £15 per pupil per annum. In future years if numbers rise with no proportionate increase in costs (and this seems likely) the unit cost will fall. A precise costing of this kind would require information on the running costs in the ILEA and in Bolton; these are not at present available.

The total cost is high and is admittedly a contrived figure which will never appear in any tangible form in either Hertfordshire or the DES. It does nevertheless represent our best estimate of the annual financial investment of the nation in the project. We have assumed in the calculation that the developmental element in the staff costs for 1977/78 will continue and that there is therefore a steady state of continuing development effort each year. Following our standard methodology, we would not capitalize this, but would write it off each year.

A calculation of unit costs at the school and authority level produces more palatable calculations. For the school it is little more than the 75 pence per pupil required to pay for the printing of worksheets by the County Reprographic Service. This is itself an artificial figure and will incorporate some subsidy elements by the county. For the county the marginal cost of continuing the HCMMP in 1978/79 could be about £6.25 per pupil per annum. This figure might be compared with the current national capitation rate for secondary schools of £16 per annum when answering the difficult value judgement: Is it worth it?

### 6. Conclusion

The HCMMP has defined its objectives as being 'to produce an all ability mathematics course for first- and second-year secondary school children and provide a computer managed system that will service that course at a reasonable cost'. The production element of this objective has been met, although the quality of the product is, as we have seen, the subject of considerable debate. The last three words of the objective are equally subjective as we face the question: what is reasonable in the context? We also find it impossible to separate neatly the costs of the course materials from those of the CML element. We are thus unable to use the project as a reliable predictor of total CML costs in isolation.

Despite these failings we hope that this case study has presented a fair picture of the largest CML project in Britain. Its achievements have been outlined, although several problems — readily acknowledged by project staff — still remain. Some of these have come to light because of the project. Among these are:

— the practical difficulties of reducing administrative chores of data handling in the classroom

— the cost and limitations of delivery systems, whether by van or on-line terminal, both of which have been shown by the project to be approximately equal in cost

— the educational problems of satisfying extremes of ability yet remaining relatively simple in structure. Will this problem ever be surmountable by standard central systems or must it be left to flexible solutions at school level?

— the technical complexity of the programming, which is harder than it seems at first sight and which will always require specialist programming assistance.

The project has started to tackle these problems and is able to claim 'a foundation of success upon which with experience, imagination and resources we can build a comprehensive model of learning and teaching within the milieu that we wish to operate'.

# Appendix C. Brief summaries of projects

This Appendix summarizes the 29 principal projects which we evaluated. It can do no more than give a very concise description of each project together with some information on its scale and quantitative achievements. Further information can be obtained from the Council for Educational Technology or by contacting the project director concerned.

Projects are described in the following order.

**Computer assisted learning projects**

1. Computer Based Learning Project (CBLP) in statistics
2. Engineering Sciences Project (ESP)
3. Computational Physics Teaching Laboratory (CPTL)
4. Clinical Decision Making
5. CAL in Chemistry (CALCHEM)
6. Mathematics Laboratory Project (MATLAB)
7. Computers in the Undergraduate Science Curriculum (CUSC)
8. Basic Mathematics at Undergraduate Level
9. CAL — A University Service
10. Management Decision Making (MDM) Project
11. CAL in Secondary School History
12. Local History Classroom Project (LHCP)
13. CAL in Upper School Geography
14. Computer Assisted Technological Education of Service Personnel
15. CAL in Nuclear Science and Technology
16. Simulation and Fault Finding on AR1 Radar (SAFARI)
17. Computer Assisted Post Office Technician Training

**Computer managed learning projects**

18. Hertfordshire Computer Managed Mathematics Project (HCMMP)
19. Computer Assisted Teaching of Remedial Reading
20. CAMOL in Secondary and Tertiary Education
21. Assessment of Student Performance and Progress
22. CAMOL in Further Education
23. Computer Assisted School Timetabling

24. Computer Scheduling of REME Training
25. Computer Aided Planning and Scheduling
26. Quality Control in Military Training

**Exchange and transfer projects**

27. Physical Sciences Program Exchange (PSPE)
28. Geographical Association Package Exchange (GAPE)
29. Havering/Lothian Transfer Project

One project, the Local Information Systems Project, was terminated very early in NDPCAL's life. Although it is included by Richard Hooper in his count of 35 projects, we have excluded it from this summary. As Appendix E points out, five other projects were not suitable for financial evaluation for one reason or another.

**1. Computer Based Learning Project (CBLP) in statistics**

*Base.* Leeds University
2 other institutions involved

| | | |
|---|---|---|
| *Estimated cost.* | NDPCAL funds | 157,000 |
| | University funds | 138,000 |
| | | £295,000 |

*Staff and student involvement.* About 1000 students from Leeds University, Bradford University and Leeds Polytechnic. 25 staff use teaching materials in 20 courses.

*Materials produced.* About 200 small modules covering different areas of statistics such as measures of location and dispersion, correlation, sampling theory. Also an author language, calculating language, and a simulation and calculating package.

*Description of use.* Used in 12 different social science disciplines with 28 terminals on four sites in the three institutions. Variety of uses: as a statistical laboratory to illustrate concepts and calculations; to teach problem solving; as an interactive example bank. It offers a support to conventional teaching with teacher and student guides prepared by the project. Most of the CAL material consists of short modules and routines which teachers group together to form their own sequences suitable for their own teaching style.

*Computer.* CTL Modular One

*Languages.* Assembler and the Leeds Author Language (LAL)

*Terminals.* Teletypes

*Period of development.* January 1973 — September 1977

*Present position.* Materials are now integrated in the statistics teaching and organized by the staff and students themselves. Students now average 8 hours per annum at terminals. The University has established three posts in the CBLP and has thus confirmed the place of CAL in the curriculum.

**2. Engineering Sciences Project (ESP)**
*Base.* Queen Mary College, University of London
5 other institutions involved

| | | |
|---|---|---|
| *Estimated cost.* | NDPCAL funds | 221,000 |
| | University funds | 178,000 |
| | | £399,000 |

*Staff and student involvement.* 10,000 student terminal hours in 1976/77 in 48 courses and six institutions. 40 academic staff actively involved.

*Materials produced.* 75 CAL packages produced, 63 in use in 1976/77. Packages have been transferred to 28 institutions outside the project.

*Description of use.* The packages deal with engineering systems which are either too complex or expensive for student experimental use but which can be simulated on the computer. Examples are: movement of electrons in an electric field; temperature distribution in a nuclear reactor. They are used interactively, in some cases replacing laboratory sessions and in others they are an extra. Some packages absorb 2-3 hours with students in groups, others are short tutorial exercises lasting about 20 minutes.

*Computers.* PDP11, PDP8, CDC 6400, Cyber 7314, Nova 2, Nova 820A, Burroughs B 6700

*Terminals.* Teletypes, Tektronix graphic display. (One institution uses computer in batch mode.)

*Languages.* FORTRAN IV, FOCAL, BASIC

*Present position.* CAL is continuing in all the member institutions. A full-time post at Queen Mary College has been funded for 21 months from 1 January 1978 by the Council for Educational Technology to coordinate the exchange and transfer of ESP packages.

**3. Computational Physics Teaching Laboratory (CPTL)**
(See Appendix A for full case study)

*Base.* Surrey University, Department of Physics

| | | |
|---|---|---|
| *Estimated cost.* | NDPCAL funds | 49,000 |
| | University funds | 87,000 |
| | | £136,000 |

*Staff and student involvement.* 5500 student hours per annum. About 18 academic staff involved.

*Materials produced.* 25 CAL packages and new or reorganized courses on computing, numerical analysis and aspects of mathematics.

*Description of use.* Varied use in dedicated CAL laboratory with 10 terminals. Timetabled use for formal courses in computing, numerical analysis and mathematics; tutorial use of CAL physics packages; free use for self-study or for project or experimental work.

*Computer.* Data General Nova 840

*Language.* BASIC

*Terminals.* Newbury VDUs

*Period of development.* October 1973 to September 1977

*Present position.* Steady state operation. Now an integral part of the department.

**4. Clinical Decision Making**
*Base.* Glasgow University
One other institution involved

| | | |
|---|---|---|
| *Estimated cost.* | NDPCAL funds | 64,000 |
| | University funds | 35,000 |
| | | £99,000 |

*Staff and student involvement.* 1300 student terminal hours in 1976/77, 4400 forecast for 1977/78

*Materials produced.* 40 units of case studies, and two general models.

*Description of use.* The long-term aim is to produce integrated courses in clinical decision-making for third-, fourth- and fifth-year clinical medicine and general practice students. Two separate models are used at present: in the 'patient management' model students work in small groups with a terminal and can compare their decisions in various areas of medicine with those of experts; in the 'emergency situation' model students work against the clock to diagnose a patient's condition. The basic models (as distinct from the data files) are content-free and can be used, for example, in police training.

*Computer.* GEC 4080

*Language.* FORTRAN IV

*Terminals.* Tektronix graphic display

*Period of development.* April 1974 — December 1977

*Present position:* The material is being adapted for use in Dundee and Leeds universities. It is used in the Glasgow Royal and Western Infirmaries and the Woodside Hospital. Computer services will continue to be provided by the University's central CAL service.

**5. CAL in Chemistry (CALCHEM)**

*Base.* Leeds University
9 other institutions involved

| | | |
|---|---|---|
| *Estimated cost.* | NDPCAL funds | 138,000 |
| | University funds | 114,000 |
| | | £252,000 |

*Staff and student involvement.* 100 teachers and 4000 students in 20 higher education institutions in the UK and abroad.

*Materials produced.* 40 packages and an author language (developed from the Leeds author language used in CBLP).

*Description of use.* There are four types of package: design of laboratory experiments; interpretation of spectra; solution of theoretical problems;

evaluation of experimental data. The computer is used via terminals mainly in a tutorial way with some calculation and simulation facilities.

*Computers.* CTL Modular One, ICL 1900, IBM 370, DEC 10, Hewlett Packard 200F, Prime 300, Burroughs B6700

*Terminals.* Teletypes

*Language.* Mainly the author language STAF, with some BASIC, FORTRAN and CALC.

*Period of development.* April 1974 — December 1977

*Present position.* The Council for Educational Technology has funded a full-time position of coordinator from 1 January 1978 to 30 September 1979. This office will be responsible for organizing the dissemination of existing CALCHEM material and for coordinating any future development activity.

**6. The MATLAB (Mathematics Laboratory) Project**

*Base.* Napier College of Commerce and Technology, Edinburgh
2 other institutions involved.

| | | |
|---|---|---|
| *Estimated cost.* | NDPCAL funds | 134,000 |
| | College funds | 133,000 |
| | | £267,000 |

*Staff and student involvement.* 550 students in 36 classes and three institutions. More than 20 staff used the materials in 1976/77.

*Materials produced.* A suite of integrated programs and routines covering the three areas of numerical analysis, matrices and statistics.

*Description of use.* Use in service mathematics teaching to students of HNC and HND in engineering and business studies. Use is via terminals with teacher supervision. The use is not tutorial CAL, but is intended to reduce the time spent on calculation and thus give more opportunity to tackle problems requiring mathematical thinking.

*Computers.* CTL Modular One, ICL 1902A, ICL 4-75, Burroughs B5700

*Terminals.* Teletypes

*Language.* FORTRAN IV

*Period of development.* December 1973 — November 1977

*Present position.* In two of the three institutions full institutionalization is claimed. Napier College will, in the short term, use the Job Creation Programme to fill two temporary positions. In the long term the College hopes that its Computer Unit will be strengthened so as to be able to offer a developed MATLAB facility.

**7. Computers in the Undergraduate Science Curriculum (CUSC)**

*Base.* University College, Queen Elizabeth and Chelsea Colleges, London, and Surrey University

| | | |
|---|---|---|
| *Estimated cost.* | NDPCAL funds | 216,000 |
| | University funds | 247,000 |
| | | £463,000 |

*Staff and student involvement.* 50 staff in 13 science departments. Over 1600 student-terminal-hours in 1976/77 with 525 students also seeing packages in lecture demonstrations.

*Materials produced.* 32 CAL packages and 2 graphics packages in Standard Fortran and Basic.

*Description of use.* Use by undergraduates in biology, chemistry, physics and statistics via terminals. The main use is the teaching of concepts by simulation allowing the student to vary parameters and investigate the consequent changes. An important aspect is the exploitation of graphics display.

*Computers.* Nova 1200, Nova 850, Elliott 4130, PDP 11, ICL 1904, ICL 1905, CDC 6400, Cyber 70, Prime 300

*Terminals.* Tektronix 4010 and Computek 300 graphics terminals

*Languages.* BASIC and FORTRAN IV

*Period of development.* January 1974 — December 1977

*Present position.* University College London is providing funds for a minicomputer which will be dedicated to CAL graphics use. Chelsea College has formed an Educational Computing Section and hopes to obtain a new minicomputer to help improve its CAL service; continuing development will be in the hands of the section. At the University of Surrey a central CAL Service (see 9) has been established.

**8. Basic Mathematics at Undergraduate Level**
*Base.* Glasgow University

| | | |
|---|---|---|
| *Estimated cost.* | NDPCAL funds | 78,000 |
| | University funds | 47,000 |
| | | £125,000 |

*Staff and student involvement.* Over 300 students in 1976/77. Student-hours expected to be over 3200 in 1977/78. 4 staff in the mathematics and physics teaching are involved.

*Materials produced.* 12 CAL units in mathematics, 7 units on physics

*Description of use.* Used in service mathematics and physics teaching for first-year undergraduates and college students in a tutorial mode unsupervised at terminals. CAL is used to give students practice in a dynamic situation by varying parameters on terminals, often using graphic display.

*Computers.* GEC 4080, Interdata 7/32

*Terminals.* Tektronix 4010 and Computek 300 graphics, GEC VDUs

*Language.* MALT (a mathematics author language) which has an interpreter written in FORTRAN IV.

*Period of development.* January 1974 — November 1977

*Present position.* A central university CAL service will continue to be used by the two departments, although development of materials will slow down.

**9. CAL — A University Service**
*Base.* Surrey University

| | | |
|---|---|---|
| *Estimated cost.* | NDPCAL funds | 7,000 |
| | University and Computer Board funds | 81,000 |
| | | £88,000 |

*Staff and student involvement.* The service is exploring several new applications other than the existing commitments to the physics, biology and chemistry departments (see 3 and 7). Two additional staff are explicitly concerned with CAL.

*Description of use.* A central CAL Service has been created with funds from the Computer Board and NDPCAL providing multi-access facilities for departments.

*Computer.* Prime 300

*Terminals.* Locally developed 'Newbury/Sigma' graphics.

*Language.* BASIC and FORTRAN

*Period of development.* October 1976—December 1977

*Present position.* The project is being evaluated in December 1977 and the University will be asked to provide funds for the expansion of the terminal network.

**10. Management Decision Making**

*Base.* London Graduate School of Business Studies (LBS).

| | | |
|---|---|---|
| *Estimated cost.* | NDPCAL funds | 79,000 |
| | LBS funds | 76,000 |
| | | £155,000 |

*Staff and student involvement.* 25 courses have been run in eight different organizations with an average class size of around 20.

*Materials produced.* 'Simulation' and 'Feedback' programs allowing conceptual models to be developed. A simple user language 'NIPPER'.

*Description of use.* Computer-based simulation of various industries and case studies are used in management training courses, either in commercial organizations or in LBS. The object is to give the managers an insight into their decision-making processes and to enable them to test their understanding of others' processes. Use of the programs in case studies can take up to two-and-a-half days in a course.

*Computer.* Hewlett Packard 2000F

*Language.* BASIC

*Terminals.* Teletype

*Period of development.* February 1975 — December 1977

*Present position.* The programs are fully developed and current work is concentrating on educational development. Ten institutions are interested in using the programs. The project director is seeking funds for a further two years' work to complete development. This will probably be based at LBS, although the school has not established a post in connection with the project.

**11. CAL in Secondary School History**
*Base.* Clwyd Education Authority

| | | |
|---|---|---|
| *Estimated cost.* | NDPCAL funds | 12,000 |
| | Local authority funds | 9,000 |
| | | £21,000 |

*Staff and student involvement.* 20 teachers and 1150 pupils are expected to be involved in 1977/78.

*Materials produced.* A working system on census returns and some development work on two other systems.

*Description of use.* The systems can be used interactively or in batch mode where large outputs are required. The census package stores the results of nineteenth-century censuses for the area and supplies lists and counts as required for classroom use. Two other packages, one supplying statements by historians on particular topics, periods and locations, and the other supplying references to resources on different topics, are not yet fully developed.

*Computers.* ICL 1903 and ICL 1901T

*Language.* PLAN

*Terminals.* Teletypes

*Period of development.* January 1976 — December 1976

*Present position.* No local authority funding is available for further development, but the census system will be used and the teachers involved will attempt to continue to develop the other systems in their own time.

**12. Local History Classroom Project (LHCP)**
*Base.* Suffolk County Council

| | | |
|---|---|---|
| *Estimated cost.* | NDPCAL funds | 42,000 |
| | Local authority funds | not available |
| | | £42,000 |

*Staff and student involvement.* In 1976/77 55 pupils used the system in eight schools and one adult education class.

*Materials produced.* A computerized data base holding about 12,000 records from nineteenth-century census returns for Suffolk towns and villages. Also teaching packages and materials for classroom use.

*Description of use.* The data base is used in batch mode with the ICL information retrieval package FIND. The application is as a teaching resource for classes in local history in secondary schools. Pupils and teachers participate in both the development and use of the data base. Schools in Dudley are also using Suffolk materials and four other institutions have requested tapes of census material.

*Computer.* ICL 1903

*Period of development.* December 1974 — December 1977

*Present position.* In the year 1977/78 between 500 and 1000 questions are expected to be processed by the system. No full-time post is being funded by the county council, although the work will receive strong support from staff of the education office.

**13. CAL in Upper School Geography**
*Base.* Birmingham University

| | | |
|---|---|---|
| *Estimated cost.* | NDPCAL funds | 40,000 |
| | University funds | 6,000 |
| | | £46,000 |

*Materials produced.* 19 units of upper secondary school geography teaching material, and another 26 in progress.

*Description of use.* Each unit is suitable for 1-3 hours of sixth-form work. Subjects covered include: 'Cities', 'Drainage Basins', 'People and Work'. Each unit comprises teachers' notes, student instructions and exercises, several alternative sets of data and computer-produced maps, diagrams and tables. The printouts are produced by the project team using data bases of census and other data. As far as teachers and pupils are concerned the use of the material is independent of the computer and no understanding of, or access to, an installation is required.

*Computer.* ICL 1906A

*Period of development.* January 1976 — December 1977

*Present position.* Remaining units are being completed and the system tested using students from Birmingham schools. A post of program analyst is being funded to September 1979 and it is likely that the material will eventually be published commercially.

**14. Computer Assisted Technological Education of Service Personnel**
*Base.* Royal Military College of Science, Shrivenham (RMCS)

| | | |
|---|---|---|
| *Estimated cosst.* | NDPCAL funds | 25,000 |
| | MOD funds | 40,000 |
| | | £65,000 |

*Staff and student involvement.* In 1977/78 seven staff will use CAL packages in five courses involving about 70 students. About 100 students will also meet packages in lectures.

*Materials produced.* 13 CAL packages (not all with NDPCAL funds) are completed now, a further 6 are being developed.

*Description of use.* CAL packages allow electrical engineering students to develop, exercise and test their knowledge of topics introduced in lectures. Students work at terminals in pairs. There is also CCTV use of packages for large lecture demonstrations of responses to parameter changes.

*Computer.* PDP 11/40

*Language:* BASIC

*Terminals.* Tektronix graphic display and VDU terminals used together.

*Period of development.* December 1975 — November 1977

*Present position.* Activity will continue after January 1978 with further developments funded by RMCS.

**15. CAL in Nuclear Science and Technology**
*Base.* Royal Naval College, Greenwich (RNCG)

| | | |
|---|---|---|
| *Contractors.* | F International Ltd | |
| Estimated cost. | NDPCAL funds | 10,000 |
| | College funds | 18,000 |
| | | £28,000 |

*Staff and student involvement.* About 50 students a year will be involved on 3 courses in 1978. Four academic staff are connected with the project.

*Materials produced.* Four large CML packages developed at RNCG by FI and two transferred from Queen Mary College (see project 2).

*Description of use.* The packages are used to simulate complex systems in nuclear design studies; students operate either singly or in pairs and are supervised by staff during tutorial time. This requires extra staff contact time.

*Computer.* Prime 400

*Language.* FORTRAN IV

*Terminals.* Tektronix graphics, teletypes

*Period of development.* January 1976 — December 1977

*Present position.* The transfer of CAL material from QMC is not yet wholly successful and the difficulties have shown that transfers of packages do not always save time. Teaching use and evaluation of RNCG packages will continue during 1978. If these prove to be successful further developments are expected to follow.

**16. SAFARI (Simulation and Fault Analysis for Radionics Instruction)**
*Base* No 1 Radio School, RAF Locking

| | | |
|---|---|---|
| *Estimated cost.* | NDPCAL funds | 24,000 |
| | MOD funds | 31,000 |
| | | £55,000 |

*Student involvement.* About 70-80 trainees per year are expected to use the system for AR1 radar (over 40 have already used it on a trial basis).

*Materials produced.* A basic 'interpreter' software system; 40 units of AR1 fault simulation; 'constructor' software to assist in building further units.

*Description of use.* Giving simulated experience in fault finding for technician training. The aims are to partly replace the real equipment by the computer (and thus make savings in the cost of hardware) and, if possible, to improve the quality of training. The system is being tested on AR1 radar, but is general in its design and could be used with other electronic equipment training.

*Computer.* PRIME 300

*Language.* FORTRAN IV

*Terminals.* Linwood VDUs

*Period of development.* May 1976 — December 1977

*Present position.* Trial system undergoing evaluation within the RAF.

**17. Computer Assisted Post Office Technician Training**
*Base.* Post Office Telecommunications Headquarters, London

| | | |
|---|---|---|
| *Estimated cost.* | NDPCAL funds | 14,000 |
| | PO funds | 28,000 |
| | | £42,000 |

*Materials produced.* A system to manage students' paths through a course on the maintenance of subscribers' equipment.

*Description of use.* The material was developed to evaluate the use of computer assisted training of maintenance engineers. Four courses have been run using the material and have been compared with conventional courses. The system provides simulation of selected fault conditions over VDUs, directs students to practical work on real equipment and provides information on student history for teaching staff.

*Computer.* IBM 370/158

*Terminals.* IBM 3271 VDUs

*Language.* Coursewriter II under the IBM Interactive Training System (ITS)

*Period of development.* August 1975 — August 1976

*Present position.* In the trial student attainment was indistinguishable from that on parallel conventional courses and progress was more rapid in the theoretical parts of the training. Further tests are planned for higher grade technicians whose courses have a higher theory content.

**18. Hertfordshire Computer Managed Mathematics Project (HCMMP)**
(See Appendix B)

*Base.* Hertfordshire County Council Advisory Unit for Computer Based Education. ILEA and Bolton also involved.

| | | |
|---|---|---|
| *Estimated cost.* | NDPCAL funds | 142,000 |
| | Local authority funds | 70,000 |
| | | £212,000 |

*Staff and student involvement.* 3000 pupils and 77 teachers in 12 Hertfordshire schools; also three Inner London Education Authority schools are using the system in 1977/78.

*Materials produced.* A complete mathematics course for the first two years of secondary school with booklets, worksheets, teachers' guides and TV programmes. Two suites of computer programs.

*Description of use.* The schools use the system either via batch processing with a courier service or by terminal over Post Office lines. The ESYMRK suite marks, assesses, routes, keeps records and provides feedback and reports to pupils and teachers. The SAM system in addition generates an arithmetic test sheet geared to the individual needs of the pupil. The course is intended for use in mixed-ability teaching.

*Computers.* Digital DEC 1050 and NCR Century 201

*Language.* COBOL

*Period of development.* October 1973 — August 1977

*Present position.* In regular use in Hertfordshire with local authority funding assured until August 1978. The system is in a steady state, but further standards will gradually be added to the SAM system and worksheets will be revised and extended.

**19. Computer Assisted Teaching of Remedial Reading**

*Base.* South Glamorgan Teachers Centre, Cardiff

| | | |
|---|---|---|
| *Estimated cost.* | NDPCAL funds on this and preceding design studies | 160,000 |
| | Local authority funds | not available |
| | | £160,000 |

*Staff and student involvement.* Piloted with 60 children from five junior schools in South Glamorgan.

*Materials produced.* A complete package of audio-visual and other teaching materials as 'tasks' made up in bags for 13 classrooms. (Some 800 tasks per class.)

*Description of use.* The computer was expected to manage the provision of remedial reading materials for up to 3 hours a week for 350 children in the first year of junior school. After a series of tests had assessed each child's abilities, the computer would be used to route each pupil through the materials and would provide the teacher with schedules of tasks required in each class. The educational design was extremely complex since it was tackling new areas of understanding about reading and learning skills.

*Computer.* ICL 1904S

*Language.* COBOL

*Terminals.* Teletypes

*Period of development.* October 1974 — December 1976

*Present position.* The project formally terminated after its mid-term evaluation but South Glamorgan was offered the project's materials to form the basis of a county resources service. NDPCAL continued to fund one post to make this possible until August 1977.

**20. CAMOL in Secondary and Tertiary Education**

*Base.* New University of Ulster (NUU)
2 other institutions involved

| | | |
|---|---|---|
| *Estimated cost.* | NDPCAL funds | 92,000 |
| | Institutional funds | 59,000 |
| | | £151,000 |

*Staff and student involvement.* So far eight staff and 400 students at NUU, and seven staff and 140 students at Methodist College, Belfast.

*Materials produced.* New or revised material for five course units in the Education Centre of NUU. 39 modules partly developed at Methodist College.

*Description of use.* Development or adaptation of ICL's CAMOL package to modules of degree and certificate courses in the Education Centre for self-teaching, multi-resource based use with varying degrees of routing and marking. Development of A-level physics self-teaching units based on commercial material at Methodist College. Development of a macro-CAMOL application at Ulster College which will assist administrative and registration functions.

*Computer.* ICL 1903A

*Language.* COBOL

*Period of development.* December 1975 — November 1977

*Present position.* The NUU and Methodist College material are in use and the macro-CAMOL is being developed and is expected to be tried during 1977-78.

**21. Assessment of Student Performance and Progress**
*Base.* Brighton Polytechnic

| | | |
|---|---|---|
| *Estimated cost.* | NDPCAL funds | 25,000 |
| | Local authority funds | 30,000 |
| | | £55,000 |

*Staff and student involvement.* About 35 staff and 600-700 students expected to be involved to some extent during 1977-78.

*Materials produced.* The test marking and analysis suite of the CAMOL system and test questions for the first year of the combined studies BSc in applied science.

*Description of use.* Application of the CAMOL CML system to various courses in the institution. Particular areas of application are in computer test marking and examination analysis; maintaining student records; preparing staff and student reports, particularly for courses involving many lecturers or several subjects.

*Computer.* ICL 1904A (polytechnic central installation)

*Language.* COBOL

*Period of development.* September 1975 — December 1977

*Present position.* CAMOL suite loaded and tested. First 'live' use of the system on six courses planned for 1977-8 academic year.

**22. CAMOL in Further Education**

*Base.* Bradford College

| | | |
|---|---|---|
| *Estimated cost.* | NDPCAL funds | 12,000 |
| | Local authority funds | 18,000 |
| | | £30,000 |

*Staff and student numbers.* About ten staff (including lecturers at neighbouring colleges and computing support) and 450 students.

*Materials produced.* Restructured units and pre- and post-testing material based on commercial self-teaching material.

*Description of use.* Application of CAMOL to craft-level students using highly structured programmed learning materials in mathematics; purpose is to provide better control and assessment of performance and faster feedback, and also to validate the material for craft-level use.

*Computer.* ICL 1906A (Bradford City Treasurer's Department)

*Period of development.* October 1976 — December 1977

*Present position.* CAMOL suite loaded and tested; educational material restructured and hand tested for craft mathematics course; 'live' trials started in autumn term 1977.

**23. Computer Assisted School Timetabling**

*Base.* Local Authorities Management Services and Computer Committee (LAMSAC)

| | | |
|---|---|---|
| *Estimated cost.* | NDPCAL funds | 41,000 |
| | LAMSAC funds | 16,000 |
| | | £57,000 |

*Description.* The project was set up to evaluate the main commercial systems that are available for producing school timetables by computer and to recommend future investment or development.

*Computers.* The NORDATA system (marketed by the Royal Institute for Public Administration) is available for Univac 1108, and IBM and ICL versions are being prepared. The OSA system (from Oxford Systems Associates Ltd) is available for ICL 1906A and DEC PDP10. The SPL system (marketed by NCC) is available for ICL 1905F, IBM 370/135, IBM 370/145, Interdata 7/32.

*Languages.* NORDATA is in FORTRAN with some assembler. OSA is in FORTRAN. SPL is in FORTRAN and COBOL.

*Period of funding.* January 1976 — December 1977

*Present position.* Surveys have been carried out of all schools using the systems and comparative trials have been performed with three systems each at three schools. A great deal of evidence has been collected on the advantages and drawbacks of each system and on resource implications; the project's report will be widely disseminated to interested authorities.

**24. Computer Scheduling of REME Training**

*Base.* School of Electrical and Mechanical Engineering, Bordon

*Contractor.* Oxford Systems Associates Ltd (OSA)

| | | |
|---|---|---|
| *Estimated cost.* | NDPCAL funds | 32,000 |
| | No matched funding | |
| | | £32,000 |

*Material produced.* Modified version of Oxford Systems Associates' scheduling package.

*Description of use.* Intended to use the computer to produce schedules for a period of about a year head of the various courses run at the School; the object was to improve on the present manual methods by achieving a less variable demand on resources and hence make savings in staff and equipment.

*Computer.* ICL 1906

*Language.* ALGOL 68

*Period of development.* January 1975 — December 1976

*Present position.* OSA's scheduling package was adapted and tested using data provided by the School. The Army have decided not to pursue the OSA approach any further at this stage, but the RAF are engaged in a similar project (25).

**25. Computer Aided Planning and Scheduling**

*Base.* No 1 Radio School, RAF Locking

*Contractor.* Oxford Systems Associates Ltd (OSA)

*Estimated cost.* NDPCAL funds £6000

Matched funding by Ministry of Defence unquantified. Consists of part of the time of management and computing staff, and computer time at RAF Locking.

*Description of use.* See 24

*Computer.* PRIME 300 using CORAL 66 at RAF Locking

*Period of development.* March — December 1977

*Present position.* Oxford Systems Associates Ltd are assisting in the design of a management information system and modifying their scheduling algorithm to suit the Locking conditions. To allow it to operate on the School's data base files they are recoding it in CORAL 66. It was planned to test it first in the autumn of 1977, and some further MOD funding is assured for the period after NDPCAL's involvement ceases.

**26. Quality Control in Military Training**

*Base.* Trade Training School, 8th Signal Regiment, Catterick Garrison

| | | |
|---|---|---|
| *Estimated cost.* | NDPCAL funds | 22,000 |
| | MOD funds | 83,000 |
| | | £105,000 |

The MOD figure includes the purchase of a dedicated computer.

*Student numbers.* There will be a gradual progress, depending on the success of the project, with a potential in the School at Catterick of about 1000 at one time or 4000 per annum.

*Description of use.* The aim is to use a CML system to manage the courses run at the Trade Training School. The areas of application are in computer test marking and question analysis, maintaining records of student progress and reporting to staff.

*Computer.* ICL 2903

*Language.* COBOL

*Period of development.* January 1976 — December 1977

*Present position.* Available CML systems have been evaluated and CAMOL chosen. The suite has been loaded and tested on a newly purchased computer. Special file and reporting systems have been developed to interface with CAMOL, and the training requirements have been appraised and respecified where necessary. A trial period started in late 1977 and, if successful, it will be extended from the beginning of 1979 to include all the School's courses.

**27. Physical Sciences Program Exchange (PSPE)**
*Base.* The Polytechnic, Wolverhampton

| | | |
|---|---|---|
| *Estimated cost.* | NDPCAL funds | 11,000 |
| | Polytechnic funds | 8,000 |
| | | £19,000 |

*Description of use.* The Exchange accepts computer programs for teaching purposes from its members, tests them, amends them where necessary and includes them in its library and catalogue. Other members can ask for programs which interest them and receive documentation and a punch card or paper tape version of the program.

*Period of development.* April 1975 — December 1977

*Present position.* Over 50 members, mainly universities and polytechnics, who provide a current demand for about 40 programs a month. The eventual aim is to make the Exchange self-supporting financially, but more members are required before this can be achieved. From January 1977 to September 1979 two part-time staff are being funded to continue the work of the Exchange.

**28. Geographical Association Package Exchange (GAPE)**
*Base.* Loughborough University

| | | |
|---|---|---|
| *Estimated cost.* | NDPCAL funds | 20,000 |
| | No significant matched funding | |
| | | £20,000 |

*Materials produced.* 12 packages catalogued and five in process.

*Description of use.* The Exchange accepts packages intended for CAL use in secondary school geography with a quantitative bias. It tests them and makes them available to secondary schools through a network of universities, polytechnics and colleges established with the Geographical Association. Schools need to have the facilities of a local computer to use the packages.

*Computers.* ICL 1904S and CTL Modular One

*Languages.* BASIC and FORTRAN IV

*Period of development.* January 1976 — December 1977

*Present position.* 270 packages have so far been requested and distributed to 70 schools and other institutions. Work of expanding the catalogue and membership will continue. External funding has been provided by CET for the period of January 1978 to September 1979.

**29. Havering/Lothian Transfer Project**
*Bases.* Educational Computing Centre, London Borough of Havering
Moray House College of Education, Edinburgh

| | | |
|---|---|---|
| *Estimated cost.* | NDPCAL funds | 16,000 |
| | Havering/Lothian funds | 16,000 |
| | | £32,000 |

*Staff and student involvement.* About five teachers and 150 pupils have used the material in schools in Lothian to test the new program material.

*Materials produced.* A translation into a very transportable version of FORTRAN of the Havering CML system.

*Description.* The Havering CML system was originally written in ALGOL and its most important application so far is in secondary level biology in Havering schools. The project aimed to produce a FORTRAN version and to test the transferability of the system software by running it on the Moray House computer to serve schools in Lothian.

*Computers.* Hewlett Packard 2116C using ALGOL, at Havering. Interdata 7/32 using FORTRAN, at Moray House.

*Period of development.* July 1975 — December 1977

*Present position.* The project has been successfully completed. The FORTRAN version of Havering's system will greatly increase the scope of its transfer to other authorities.

# Appendix D. Documents used in the evaluation

In this appendix we reproduce some of the pro-forma and documents that were used in evaluation for the benefit of those readers who are interested in our methodology. Chapter 3 has explained this in outline, but the documents illustrate more effectively the detailed data with which we were concerned. We show them in the chronological order in which they were written.

**Appendix D.1. Checklist of data needed**

This is the revised version of a standard document sent to all project directors as soon as their project had been approved. It represented our understanding of our data needs. We visited each director to talk over the checklist, modify it in the light of his special circumstances and discuss how he might set up data collection systems to answer the questions we had posed.

**Appendix D.2. Analyses of academic staff time**

The data area which gave the greatest cause for concern was that related to academic staff time. Project directors felt no compunction asking NDPCAL employees to complete time records, but hesitated to bully academic colleagues, whom they were in some instances trying to tempt into sampling CAL. One project needed our help in clarifying the objectives of the exercise. Appendix D.2 was written for their benefit, but is valuable as it describes the practice adopted by the major projects in providing information on the academic staff involvement.

**Appendix D.3. The final stages**

After the mid-term evaluation meetings most projects were confirmed for an extended period of funding. There was a danger that project directors might relax their efforts on data collection now that the hurdle had been cleared. To counter this the Final Stages memorandum was sent to directors after their project had been approved. As well as reminding them of the continuing data requirements, it points out four particular areas of concern.

**Appendices D.4 and D.5. Final Review of projects 1977**

In April and May 1977 the one-day Final Review meetings were held for 13 projects. One of the sessions was devoted to financial and resource issues. In order to concentrate on the discussion and to provide some comparability between answers and a basis for NDPCAL-wide generalizations project directors were sent a list of topics. Appendix D.4 covered CAL projects while Appendix D.5 related to CML. The attachment to Appendix D.4 is a cost calculation sheet which showed directors how to work out the total cost of their project according to our standard methodology.

# Appendix D.1 Financial and resource evaluation: Checklist of data needed

**1. Finance**

— Records of all costs by original budget headings (giving four monthly totals).
— Actual costs borne by institution (Heads 11 to 16 for last accounting year).
— Analysis of costs by category of activity (eg, Program Development, Curriculum Development).

| | |
|---|---|
| — Computer and other stationery<br>— Printing costs<br>— Communications costs<br>— Travelling and subsistence | } only where significant. |

**2. Staff time**

*2.1 For staff funded by National Programme*

— Analysis of their time split between 4 activities — to be done monthly (± 5% tolerance) or at whatever interval seems reasonable. The four categories of activity are:
  — development time on programs and systems
  — curriculum development time
  — teaching or operating time using the new programs
  — general administrative time.

If desired, two other categories could be added: supervision time (while students are using terminals) and promotional or public relations time (explaining the project to others or assisting with its transfer elsewhere).

*2.2 For staff of the institution (academic, technical and secretarial)*

— Analysis of time split between the 4 activities — to be done at the discretion of project director to produce realistic and defensible figures — (this can be monthly or termly, in hours or percentage of time).
— An estimate of the effect of the project on staff workload. Has any element of their work expanded or contracted considerably because of the project?
— Any measurable effects on other departmental staff not working on the project.

— Any identifiable effects on the future workload of staff in the institution because of the project.
— An approximate estimate by the central financial administration of their time on the project.

**3. Course content and context**

— Are the CAL packages optional or compulsory in the course?
— What approximate proportion of the total course contact time do they take up?
— Will staff still steer or supervise students doing the packages?
— Will the content of the course be greater (or larger) as a result of the packages? (An increase in educational quality — however defined — and a stylistic change in the basic educational content have been assumed.)
— Has the introduction of the CAL packages into one part of the course affected any other part of the course in any measurable sense (eg, length).

**4. Computers and terminals**

— Summary of logged computer and terminal time by user and category of activity (and main course, where many departments are sharing a common program).
— If available a split by module, package or topic would also be interesting.
— Summary or estimate of undue burden on computer peripherals, or storage. Give any known data on core storage requirements of the programs.
— Details of any charges made by a computer centre (whether reimbursed by the National Programme or not).
— All available information on terminal usage showing numbers in use by hour of day and day of week. Also an analysis of this use by activity (eg, teaching program development). Use terminal room timetable if possible.
— Information on time spent on any dedicated computer for purposes other than the project (eg, small research jobs).

**5. Space**

— Summary and description of space wholly devoted to the project (square feet).
— Estimate of space used by project staff for the purposes of the project

with an approximate percentage of the time so used (offices, laboratories, computer rooms).
- Description of the impact of project on scheduled teaching or laboratory rooms, including an estimate of the extent to which the 'mix' of space use has altered.

**6. Student numbers**
- Give information on numbers of students using each module (or subject area) of the programs that have been developed.
- What is the total contact-time of each student for each session?
- Do they share terminals?
- Do they require supervision? If so, how often and from whom?
- Provide details of untimetabled use of programs by students.
- Have the students any knowledge of terminals or programming before they use the programs?

**7. Institutional costs**
- Where costs such as telephone, postage, stationery, insurance and staff advertising exceed £200 and can be directly identified with the project they should be stated.
- If costs cannot be clearly identified and are thought to exceed £200 per annum on any one item give a rough estimate.

**8. Other categories of resource or impact**

*8.1 Examinations*
- Has the project altered the previous examination system? Can the change be quantified?

*8.2 Books and learning resources*
- What impact if any has the project had on these? Can it be measured at all?

*8.3 Equipment for teaching*
- Will the equipment used in laboratories or classrooms be any different as a result of the project?
- Is any equipment now no longer needed? If so provide a list. Would it have a resale value?

John Fielden
Peat, Marwick, Mitchell & Co
Management Consultants
Revised 1 August 1974

# Appendix D.2. Analyses of academic staff time

**Background**

The National Development Programme is spending £2 million investigating an expensive innovation. CAL is easily avoidable since the money being spent on it could well be redirected at a time of unparalleled financial difficulty. The innovation has in public eyes all the aura of an expensive luxury. For this reason the financial evaluation of the Programme will be important.

In 1976/77 and 1977/78 the anticipated expenditure of the National Programme will be spent as follows.

| | *1976/77* | *1977/78* |
|---|---|---|
| Salaries | 64 | 69 |
| Other costs | 27 | 29 |
| Non-recurrent expenditure | 9 | 2 |
| | 100% | 100% |

Thus the great majority of the funds will be spent, rightly, on people. Attention will therefore be focused on how these people used their time. Already oversimplified questions are being asked using emotive words such as 'productivity', 'output' and 'efficient use of time'. It is the job of the financial evaluation to tackle questions such as these with a real understanding of the problems and issues involved. In other words it is hoped to provide informed answers to the questions so that naïve and oversimplified judgements are pre-empted.

**The information requirements of the National Programme**

All projects and studies commissioned by the National Programme are subject to the regulations and disciplines embodied in *Control and Reporting Systems for Development Projects*. The acceptance of these systems was a fundamental condition of the grant of funds to each institution. Appendix VI to the 'Jackdaw' describes the contents of an annual report required from all projects. Section 3 is headed 'Staffing' and asks project directors to provide approximate apportionment of time of all staff engaged on the project (full-time and part-time, whether funded by the Programme or not) during the year. An example is provided showing the time of 3 people analysed in percentage terms over 4 categories.

Following the NDP's acceptance of reporting and information requirements, the financial evaluation has been helping projects establish their own data collection systems.

**How should staff time be analysed?**

Clearly, it is impossible to produce an exact apportionment or even estimate of academic staff time spent on a CAL project. Figures supplied will therefore be 'best guesses'. The National Programme expects the individuals concerned to make these guesses since they alone are the best judge of how their time is spent. Each project director is charged with collecting the information together and with ensuring that it is reasonable and realistic in total.

From visits to projects it is clear that the obligation to collect data is being universally accepted, although obviously the mechanics of the operation vary. The financial evaluation has not so far recommended any standard system, but has left it to project directors to design the one most applicable. The variants include:

(1) detailed time analysis required for NDP-*and* institutionally-funded staff in hours of time (DP 1/07, FS 4/02, FS 1/04, FS 1/22/01)
(2) monthly estimates (as a percentage of total time) for academic staff; more detailed hourly estimates for NDP-funded staff (DP 1/04, FS 2/02)
(3) monthly estimates for NDP-funded staff, termly estimates in either hours or days as convenient for academic staff (DP 1/02 and DP 1/06)

The last of these options is thought to be the most realistic, since the termly frequency is not too great to cause irritation and yet it does allow a reasonable guess to be made of the time invested. The precise form used by one project to obtain this information is attached to this memorandum.

The main purpose of collecting staff time information is to allow informed comments to be made on the cost of CAL. If projects do not cooperate in providing such data, ill-informed and inaccurate estimates may well be made. Experience in projects so far shows that the allocation and investment of time is very different from that originally estimated (as might be expected from such an innovatory Programme).

John Fielden<br>Peat, Marwick, Mitchell & Co<br>25 November 1975

*Examples of forms used by projects are shown on pages 200 and 201.*

## Engineering Science Project in Computer Assisted Learning

Dear

In assessing the cost of development and implementation of CAL packages in the Engineering Science Project it is necessary to estimate the time spent by members of academic staff concerned, divided between the four categories of activity:

(a) curriculum development
(b) program development
(c) program implementation
(d) general administration.

I should be grateful if you would estimate the time (in hours or days, whichever you find more convenient) which you have devoted to each of these categories during the term, (including the preceding vacation where appropriate) and complete and return the attached form to me as soon as possible.

This information will be held in project records and be available to the National Programme Directorate on request.

ENGINEERING SCIENCE PROJECT

NAME ____________________
DEPARTMENT ____________________
INSTITUTION ____________________
TERM ____________________ YEAR ____________________

| CATEGORY | TIME | PACKAGE NAME OR REF. |
|---|---|---|
| curriculum development | | |
| program development | | |
| program implementation | | |
| general administration | | |
| other (specify) | | |

SIGNATURE ____________________

DATE ____________________

CALCHEM

TERMLY REPORT FORM Page 1

1. Institution

Term

Year

2. *Estimates of staff time spent this term (in hours)*

Creating the teaching plan

Programming

Supervising students (above normal)

Administration

Other, eg, dicussions, talks

3. *Student use of programs this term*

| Program No | Title | Student group | Student numbers | Total time |
|---|---|---|---|---|
| | | | | |
| | | | | |
| | | | | |
| | | | | |
| | | | | |
| | | | | |
| | | | | |

# Appendix D.3. Financial and resource evaluation: the final stages

Now that the evaluation visit is over and a first financial evaluation report has been produced, the emphasis of the evaluation will change slightly. This note aims to outline the main concerns of the financial evaluation agency between now and December 1977.

**1. Data collection and preparation (or revision) of cost statements**

One of the most important products of the evaluation will be the costings of projects. These are likely to follow the methodology outlined in Technical Report No 9 which produces data at three levels, giving the resource implications for the department, the institution and the nation. These can only be based on data produced by projects in their concluding years. It is therefore vital that the information systems which have been set up continue to operate until the end of NDP funding. The final financial evaluation of each project will take place before the end of 1977. This evaluation is likely to be independent of any review undertaken by the Programme Directorate. It will be necessary to 'draw a line' under the data collected up to a certain date and use it to calculate detailed statements of resource implications and costs. The most probable 'cut off point' for these purposes will be April 1977.

The data from the second step of projects will be more significant to the financial evaluation than that from the first step. It will gain in significance as the project nears the end of NDP funding, since in most cases this should represent the end of the development phase and the approach of a steady state situation. In practice, however, some development will continue with internal funding represented by staff time. It should, nonetheless, be possible to predict from the final years of funding the likely resource impact (in terms of direct, marginal and total costs) of CAL on the institution after the 'takeover'. This information could be of great value to committees and administrators in the institutions concerned.

**2. Generalizations on financial matters**

The second main task of the evaluation will be to produce generalizations on issues such as:

— the ranges of development time per package
— the resource implications of teletype versus graphic display terminals and of batch versus on-line use
— the effect of budgetary constraints and procedures on the adoption of CAL
— the economies to be gained from shared development of packages and inter-institutional transfers
— the effect on resource implications of CAL being an extra or a substitution in the teaching situation
— the resource implications of different uses of the computer, eg, the computer as a laboratory.

These topics will be covered in a series of 'Financial Issues Reports' and will be produced gradually between now and the end of the National Programme. In a few cases they will be based on detailed studies in some projects.

**3. Information systems in projects**

The information systems which have been established in the first step of each project centred round the following key items of data.

| | | |
|---|---|---|
| 1. | Use of CAL | — statistics on numbers of students, terminal hours, type of use. |
| 2. | Time analysis | — staff time by category of activity. |
| 3. | Computer time | — statistics on CPU time, storage used and terminal connect time. |
| 4. | Other costs | — space, overheads and direct costs. |
| 5. | Educational data | — quantifiable effects on curriculum, books, exams, etc. |
| 6. | Savings | — staff time released, any direct economies. |

In this final stage, the existing information systems should not require any major modifications. It would be helpful, however, if project directors could consider 4 points and amend their systems, if need be, in the light of this consideration.

*1. Inflation*

Are the data inflation proof? If data is being collected in cost terms, could it be in unit terms instead? For example, a charge from a printing unit of £100 might be expressed as 7500 pages of print. This latter unit is inflation proof and can be converted later into money.

*2. Educational use*

Is there adequate information on the educational use of CAL and the packages developed? It is a key point in the financial evaluation whether or not CAL is an extra or a substitution. This may involve inquiry into previous teaching methods. In many cases, however, such investigations are unnecessary if CAL is doing something educationally that was not feasible before.

*3. Cost reduction*

Are there any sources of economies in operation that the project has not taken into account? For instance, the shared use of terminals can reduce costs (and, it is claimed, can sometimes enhance the educational benefits) in relevant subject areas. Users in other institutions might take the materials developed and might decide to take advantage of some of the areas for cost-reduction.

*4. Transfers*

Are systems set up to identify the resource implications in those institutions which take on packages or material from NDP projects? In most cases it will be necessary to keep closely in touch with the recipients. Some projects have designed questionnaires which recipients are asked to complete.

Remember that if projects can claim successful transfers and collect evidence on use (in student hours) these figures can be aggregated to their own package student hours to produce lower unit costs!

The cooperation and support received from all projects has been consistent and strong. The task of the evaluation agency has been made immeasurably easier by their assistance. The need for reliable financial data will become important to university institutions as they enter the detailed debate about resource allocation in the next quinquennium. In other sectors of education calls for stringent economies may be stilled by realistic statements of marginal cost.

John Fielden
Peat, Marwick, Mitchell & Co
September 1975

# Appendix D.4. Final review of CAL projects 1977

**Items to be considered in third session. Resources and finance**

The third session will be chaired by John Fielden of PMM & Co and will cover issues relating to the financial evaluation. The format will be that projects will present their answers to a list of questions concerning financial issues. One or two of the answers will require supporting paperwork which should be tabled. There will then be a short period for discussion with the visiting evaluators.

The questions to which answers are sought (multi-institutional projects will not have uniform answers to all of them) are as follows.

1. To what extent has the computer replaced laboratory time, tutorial or examples classes?
2. Ignoring development time, has CAL increased either the student-contact time or the workload of any academic staff. If so, how much?
3. Are there any realizable economies from the introduction of CAL?
4. What *extra* costs fall on the departmental budget because of CAL?
5. What *extra* costs fall on the institutional budget?
6. What terminal utilization figures have been achieved in the last three terms (76/77 and 75/76) in student-hours per terminal? Please specify if terminals are shared and give terminal-hours also.
7. Given your timetable constraints what is the maximum possible usage per terminal per annum?
8. How long has it taken to develop packages (give programmer time and academic staff time separately if possible)?
9. Has the inter-institutional nature of the project saved you any time or resources? Can you identify any savings on packages sponsored and taken over?
10. What are the total costs of the packages (following the standard PMM methodology) developed in the project? A separate figure should be derived for each participating institution.

John Fielden
Peat, Marwick, Mitchell & Co
17 December 1976

**Cost calculation sheet (for a future hypothetical steady state situation)**

| | | | |
|---|---|---|---|
| **A.** | **Equipment** | | |
| 1. | Total capital cost of computer used | £________ | |
| 2. | Proportion of actual use on project | ________% | |
| 3. | Cost applicable to project (2 x 1) | £________ | |
| 4. | Annual depreciation (3 over 7 years) | | £________ |
| 5. | Cost of terminals used in projects | £________ | |
| 6. | Proportion of actual use on project | ________% | |
| 7. | Cost applicable to project (6 x 5) | £________ | |
| 8. | Annual depreciation (7 over 5 years) (If other equipment is used, please apply same methodology.) | | £________ |
| 9. | Total maintenance costs of computer | £________ | |
| 10. | Share borne by project (2 x 9) | | £________ |
| 11. | Total maintenance costs of terminals | £________ | |
| 12. | Share borne by project (6 x 11) | | £________ |
| 13. | Share of overheads and other remaining costs of central computer and terminals | | |
| | — rent of space (£2 or £3 per sq ft) | _____ sq ft | £________ |
| | — operational and programming staff | | £________ |
| 14. | Total equipment-related cost | | £________ |
| **B.** | **Annual running costs of project in 1977/78** | | |
| 1. | Total salary cost (including pension and NHI) of all non-academic staff engaged on project in future | £________ | |
| 2. | Proportion of total salary of all *academic* staff on project | £________ | |
| 3. | Duplication and printing costs | £________ | |
| 4. | Post Office line rental and charges | £________ | |
| 5. | Other consumable costs | £________ | |
| 6. | Rent of space used by full-time project staff | £________ | |
| 7. | Estimate of central administrative overheads related to project | £________ | |
| 8. | Total annual running costs | | £________ |

**C. Past development costs**

| | | | |
|---|---|---|---|
| 1. | Estimate (if possible) of total pre-NDP development costs | | £ ______ |
| 2. | NDP's total allocation to project | £______ | |
| 3. | Institutional 'matched funding' | £______ | |
| 4. | Total | £______ | |
| 5. | Less: Capital expenditure (in A1 and A5) | (£ ______ ) | |
| 6. | Total 4 - 5 | £______ | |
| 7. | Proportion of staff time in project related to administration and teaching | ______% | |
| 8. | Apply 7 to 6 | £______ | |
| 9. | 6 - 8 | | £ ______ |
| 10. | Total (1 + 9) | | £______ |
| 11. | Annual write off of development (20% of 10) | | £______ |
| | TOTAL OF ALL COSTS (A14 + B8 + C11) | | £______ |

# Appendix D.5. Final review of CML projects 1977

**Items to be considered in third session. Resources and finance**

The third session will be chaired by PMM & Co and will cover issues relating to the financial evaluation. The format will be that projects will present their answers to a list of questions concerning financial issues. One or two of the answers will require supporting paperwork which should be tabled. There will then be a short period for discussion with the visiting evaluators.

The questions to which answers are sought (multi-institutional projects will not have uniform answers to all of them) are as follows.

1. To what extent has the computer altered staff time previously spent on management activities? Give details of:
   — the type of staff (academic, administrative, clerical)
   — the amount of time
   — the activities (marking, student-routing, remedial direction of students, record-keeping, preparation of tests, etc)
2. What benefits does the computer produce that were not available before (more detailed records of student-performance, question analysis, etc)? Has this had any quantifiable effects in resource usage on student achievement?
3. Ignoring development costs, has CML increased the academic/administrative staff work-load in any way?
4. What student numbers are involved during 1966/7 and what is the probable future involvement in the medium and long term?
5. What extra costs fall on the departmental budget because of CML?
6. What extra costs fall on the institutional budget?
7. How long has it taken to develop the *system?* Give educational and computing development time separately and for multi-institutional projects, include only the resources of your own institution.
8. What effort is required, after the initial development, to produce course material for the system (question banks, routing details, etc)?
9. What extra staff time is required within the computer installation

or in liaison between the academic departments and the computer department? How is this dependent upon the number of students, courses or departments involved?

10. Using the PMM methodology calculate the total cost per student/pupil per annum of the system.
11. Are there any quantifiable cash savings?

Peat, Marwick, Mitchell & Co
28 February 1977

# Appendix E. Cost of the evaluation

The financial evaluation has been undertaken by professional staff of Peat, Marwick, Mitchell & Co, Management Consultants, at a cost of £62,545. This has contained three elements:

| | |
|---|---|
| Fees | 54,475 |
| Travelling and other expenses | 3,325 |
| VAT | 4,745 |
| | £62,545 |

The manpower involved represented 112 man-weeks spread over the four-and-a-half years of the evaluation.

In order to help in the planning of any later such studies we have analysed the time spent into its main categories. This shows the following spread of effort:

| | |
|---|---|
| Visits to projects (111 visits) | 30 man-weeks |
| Evaluation visits and reports | 23 man-weeks |
| Annual and final reports and publications | 25 man-weeks |
| Meetings, coordination, conferences | 18 man-weeks |
| Other activities | 16 man-weeks |
| | 112 man-weeks |

We played little or no part in four of the NDP's projects, which were for one reason or another not suitable for an evaluation. These were:

Cambridge University Transferability Project
RAF Staff College, Bracknell
BASIC to FORTRAN machine translation
CAMOL coordination

In addition some projects came to an end during NDP's life and were not included in the 35 listed by Hooper in his *Final Report.* We spent some effort on these and in the early days of our involvement on some projects which never came to fruition.

As we mention in Chapter 2, we admit that the evaluation did not have adequate manpower resources to carry out a thorough financial assessment of each project. Some were not ready for this by September 1977, but others were and we were guilty of underestimating the time required to fulfil the detailed evaluation function. Although it is unlikely that any other funding organization will exactly repeat NDPCAL's managerial activities (with the emphasis on long evaluation visits, conferences and frequent travel) we consider that if an evaluation of resources is ever required again it would need at least four weeks per project in addition to the 'overhead' element of attendance at conferences and other coordination sessions.

# Appendix F. References


**Publications from the financial evaluation**

FIELDEN, J (1974) 'The financial evaluation of CAL projects', *International Journal of Mathematical Education in Science and Technology,* **5**, 4

FIELDEN, J (1975) 'An approach to measuring the cost of computer assisted learning', Technical Report No 9. NDPCAL, London

PEARSON, P K (1976) 'Cost of conventional teaching in universities', Technical Report No 13. NDPCAL, London

FIELDEN, J (1977a) 'The financial evaluation of NDPCAL', *British Journal of Educational Technology,* **8**, 3

PEARSON, P K (1977) *Costs of education in the United Kingdom.* Council for Educational Technology, London

FIELDEN, J (1977b) 'Chapter 4. The costs of CAL'. In the *Final Report of the Director, NDPCAL.* Council for Educational Technology, London

FIELDEN, J (1978) 'Chapter 10. Counting the cost'. In *Interactive computer graphics in science teaching,* ed J McKenzie. Ellis-Horwood, Chichester

**Other references**

CARNEGIE COMMISSION ON HIGHER EDUCATION (1972) *The fourth revolution.* McGraw-Hill, New York

DUNWORTH, J (1974) 'Undergraduate laboratory utilization and requirements', *British Journal of Educational Technology,* **3**, 5

FIELDEN, J (1978) 'The cost of innovation and change in education', *Programmed Learning and Educational Technology,* **15**, 3

FIELDEN, J and PEARSON, P K (1978) *Costing educational practice.* Council for Educational Technology, London

FIELDEN, J and LOCKWOOD, G (1973) *Planning and management in universities.* Chatto and Windus, London

HOOPER, R (1975) *Two years on. NDPCAL. Report of the Director.* Council for Educational Technology, London

HOOPER, R (1977) *Final report of the Director. NDPCAL.* Council for Educational Technology, London

HOOPER, R (1978) 'Some new approaches to research and development funding', *Higher Education,* **7**, 1

JAMISON, D, KLEES, S and WELLS, S (1976) *Cost analysis for educational planning and methodology and application to instructional technology.* Educational Testing Service, Princeton, N J

KEMMIS, S (1977) *The educational potential of computer assisted learning: qualitative evidence about student learning.* Centre for Applied Research in Education, University of East Anglia

LAYARD, R (1973) 'New media and higher education', *Minerva,* **XI**, 2

MILES, R (1977) 'Computers in military training in the 1980s. A future study report', Technical Report No 18. NDPCAL, London

MILES, R (1977a) 'Computer assisted learning in the services', *Services Education,* 3

NCET (1969) *Computers for education,* (Working Paper 1). National Council for Educational Technology, London

PETERSON, J (1977) 'The typical CAL program', *CALNEWS 8.* NDPCAL, London

SHIRLEY, R (1978) In J McKenzie, ed, *Interactive computer graphics in science teaching.* Ellis-Horwood, Chichester

UNCAL (1975) *The programme at two.* Centre for Applied Research in Education, University of East Anglia

UNESCO (1977) *The economics of new educational media.* UNESCO, Paris